P9-CCP-346

Teacher Leadership

That Strengthens Professional Practice

Charlotte Danielson

Association for Supervision and Curriculum Development
Alexandria, Virginia USA

ASCD®

Association for Supervision and Curriculum Development
1703 N. Beauregard St. • Alexandria, VA 22311-1714 USA
Phone: 800-933-2723 or 703-578-9600 • Fax: 703-575-5400
Web site: www.ascd.org • E-mail: member@ascd.org
Author guidelines: www.ascd.org/write

Gene R. Carter, *Executive Director*; Nancy Modrak, *Director of Publishing*; Julie Houtz, *Director of Book Editing & Production*; Darcie Russell, *Project Manager*; Greer Beeken, *Graphic Designer*; Keith Demmons, *Desktop Publishing Specialist*; Dina Seamon, *Production Specialist/Team Lead*

All Web links in this book are correct as of the publication date below but may have become inactive or otherwise modified since that time. If you notice a deactivated or changed link, please e-mail books@ascd.org with the words "Link Update" in the subject line. In your message, please specify the Web link, the book title, and the page number on which the link appears.

ASCD Member Book, No. FY06-05 (February 2006, P). ASCD Member Books mail to Premium (P), Comprehensive (C), and Regular (R) members on this schedule: Jan., PC; Feb., P; Apr., PCR; May, P; July, PC; Aug., P; Sept., PCR; Nov., PC; Dec., P.

PAPERBACK ISBN-13: 978-1-4166-0271-2   ASCD product #105048
PAPERBACK ISBN-10: 1-4166-0271-2
e-book editions: retail PDF ISBN-13: 978-1-4166-0331-3; retail PDF ISBN-10: 1-4166-0331-X •
netLibrary ISBN-13: 978-1-4166-0329-0; netLibrary ISBN-10: 1-4166-0329-8 •
ebrary ISBN-13: 978-1-4166-0330-6; ebrary ISBN-10: 1-4166-0330-1

Quantity discounts for the paperback edition only: 10–49 copies, 10%; 50+ copies, 15%; for 500 or more copies, call 800-933-2723, ext. 5634, or 703-575-5634. For desk copies: member@ascd.org.

Library of Congress Cataloging-in-Publication Data

Danielson, Charlotte.
 Teacher leadership that strengthens professional practice / Charlotte Danielson.
     p. cm.
 Includes bibliographical references and index.
 ISBN-13: 978-1-4166-0271-2 (alk. paper)
 ISBN-10: 1-4166-0271-2 (alk. paper)

 1. Teacher participation in administration. 2. Teachers--Professional relationships. 3. Educational leadership. I. Title.
 LB2806.45.D36   2006
 371.1 ·06--dc22
                        2005027510

13 12 11 10 09 08 07 06   12 11 10 9 8 7 6 5 4 3 2 1

To Teacher Leaders and Their Administrators

The framework for teacher leadership is the culmination of many years' work in education and is a result of a growing recognition that the work of many teachers is not fully encompassed in descriptions of *teaching*. Even the framework for teaching, used in many school districts and states throughout the United States and overseas, does not completely capture the work of the most advanced, experienced, and expert professional teachers. For them, and for all teachers who strive to extend their influence beyond their immediate teaching responsibilities, a larger description is needed. These are teacher *leaders*, professional educators who don't want to become administrators, but whose work extends beyond their own students.

As has been well documented, the work of teaching is extremely complex and challenging on a minute-to-minute basis. Teachers must possess strength and resilience to meet that challenge every day, under, in some cases, most difficult working conditions. And yet they do—they go to work every day and make a difference for the children in their charge.

In addition, some of those teachers go the extra mile and find ways to extend their influence beyond the students they teach. They recognize opportunities to improve their schools, and they seize those opportunities, going well beyond the basic responsibilities of their positions. These teachers are not ambitious in the traditional way; they do not seek to become administrators. Rather, they are committed to teaching, and they retain teaching well as their primary goal. But they also recognize that they have more to offer the profession if they extend their gaze beyond the walls of their own classrooms and initiate projects that will improve the educational program for all students in their school and perhaps for students beyond that boundary.

These are the teacher leaders, and it is to them, and the administrators who support their work, that I dedicate this book.

Teacher Leadership

That Strengthens Professional Practice

Acknowledgments vi

Part I: Teacher Leadership: Breaking New Ground
1: Leadership Stories 3
2: What Is Teacher Leadership? .12
3: What Do Teacher Leaders Do? 28
4: School Culture 45

Part II: How Teacher Leadership Is Demonstrated
5: Schoolwide Policies and Programs 61
6: Teaching and Learning 84
7: Communications and Community Relations 105

Part III: Promoting and Developing Teacher Leadership
8: Promoting Teacher Leadership 125
9: The Skills of Teacher Leadership 133

Appendix: School Audit 147
References 154
Index 156
About the Author 160

Acknowledgments

My interest in the systematic concept of teacher leadership arose from a project in which I was peripherally involved, in the state of Victoria, in Australia. The administration of the sector of Catholic schools there was interested in enticing teachers into the ranks of administration and recognized that many teachers did not have a full appreciation of whether such work would appeal to them. They proposed the development of a structure to describe the leadership opportunities that presented themselves to teachers who might want to become school principals.

When I returned to the United States, I discovered considerable interest in the topic of teacher leadership, but not as a precursor to administration. Rather, many educators expressed intense interest in teacher leadership as exercised by teachers whose professional goals do not include moving into administration. Those educators recognize that the work of administrators is fundamentally different from that of teachers, and while they want to extend their reach beyond the students they teach every day, they want their responsibilities to be essentially those of teachers.

Following months of conversations with educators all around the United States, I drafted a framework for teacher leadership, trying to capture the best of what I had learned from this dialogue. The result is described in this book, *Teacher Leadership That Strengthens Professional Practice*. Following its drafting, and prior to its submission to

ASCD, many of the individuals with whom I had spoken were generous with their time and provided most valuable comments and suggestions. I gratefully acknowledge their contribution.

To the following individuals I am particularly grateful:

Lawrence Ingvarson and Elizabeth Kleinhenz, of the Australian Council for Educational Research, in Melbourne, Australia, for the initial opportunity to explore the concept of teacher leadership;

Marilyn Schlief, of the Michigan Education Association, for convening a session of teachers and administrators to provide feedback on the initial framework;

Margaret Holtschlag for contributing the story about the BIG Lesson and commenting on a draft of its description;

Barb Meloche for contributing the story about looping and commenting on a draft of its description;

Kendra Hearn, Jim Linsell, and Olga Moir for contributing their experiences to the concept of teacher leadership;

Vivienne Collinson for her groundbreaking work on the concept of teacher leadership;

Kristina Hesbol, Steve McKibben, Candi McKay, Lynn Sawyer, and Karyn Wright for reading and providing extensive comments on earlier drafts of the manuscript;

Thousands of educators with whom I have spoken at conferences and meetings since 2003 on the evolution of the concept of teacher leadership, and who have made innumerable suggestions for its refinement.

I consider this framework for teacher leadership to be a collective product of many, *many* educators as they have engaged with the concept and contributed to its development. Thank you.

Part I

Teacher Leadership: Breaking New Ground

The concept of teacher leadership is not new; indeed, every educator has encountered colleagues whom they would describe as leaders, individuals to whom they look for professional advice and guidance, and whose views matter to others in the school. The educational literature on teacher leadership is, furthermore, fairly extensive. To this point, however, the critical characteristics of teacher leaders, as distinct from teachers who are assigned to leadership positions, has not been fully described. This book fills that void and is offered in recognition that many teachers don't regard teacher leadership as a stepping stone toward administration; rather it represents its own way of working in schools and making a contribution to student learning.

The principal characteristic of teacher leadership, as described here, is that it is completely *informal*. Teacher leaders don't gain their authority through an assigned role or position; rather, they *earn* it through their work with both their students and their colleagues. Teacher leaders play a highly significant role in the work of the school and in school improvement efforts. Precisely because of its informal and voluntary nature, teacher leadership represents the highest level of professionalism. Teacher leaders are not being paid to do their work; they go the extra mile out of a commitment to the students they serve.

Part I begins with three stories of teachers who illustrate these characteristics. Subsequent chapters describe teacher leadership in some detail and enumerate what it is that teacher leaders actually do. In other words, what do teacher leaders do that is different from the work of excellent teachers who are not teacher leaders? Lastly, Part I concludes with a discussion of the critical matter of school culture and the impact it has not only on what teacher leaders do, but also on how they do it.

1

Leadership Stories

The term "teacher leadership," which has been much in the professional news of late, has been used in a number of different senses. Its meaning, as used in this book, is best illustrated by three examples.

A New Way to Do Field Trips

In 1997, Margaret[1], a 4th grade teacher in Michigan, took her students (as she had for many years) on a field trip to the local historical museum. The outing was fairly typical of such excursions: some preparation for what the children might see, a lot of "herding" by Margaret, a few parent volunteer chaperones, and children attempting to conceal (not very successfully) their boredom with presentations by the museum staff. In fact, Margaret remembers, the children exhibited "considerably more motivation for spending their money at the museum gift shop than learning about Michigan's history."

By the next year, things had changed. Margaret was dissatisfied with the quality of the learning in which her students were engaged. In fact, she was beginning to wonder whether the annual field trip was a wise expenditure of the district's scarce resources. So

---

[1] All the teachers described in this chapter are based on real individuals. Margaret's story describes a project created by Margaret Holtschlag, a teacher in Haslett, Michigan. The project is now supported by the Michigan Department of Education and the Michigan Council for Arts and Cultural Affairs, and sample lessons are available at www.biglesson.org. Elena's story is an adaptation of an authentic situation. Tom's account is a composite of several different people.

she arranged to meet with the education staff at the museum to consider alternatives. The result was the BIG History Lesson, in which Margaret's 4th graders spent an *entire week* at the museum!

Naturally, such an effort required a lot of planning, including meeting with the staff at the museum, locating a room the class could use for the week, and arranging for transportation and parent helpers each day, to say nothing of structuring the week's activities to take full advantage of the many resources of the museum.

The concept has been extended since 1998 to include the BIG Zoo Lesson, the BIG Nature Lesson, the BIG Science lesson, and the BIG Culture Lesson, reaching 2,500 Michigan students in grades 1–8 from 12 districts in 2004–05. While at an off-campus site, students participate in lessons particular to that site and integrate work in language arts, mathematics, science, and history. Moreover, students engage in daily reflection on their activities, partly for closure and partly to structure the next day's activities.

One of the greatest benefits reported by both teachers and students is the opportunity for in-depth work. For example, in the BIG Zoo Lesson, students observe a single animal each day for a week, exploring such concepts as group behavior, camouflage, eating and sleeping habits, and use of tools. Such sustained focus is simply impossible in a traditional trip to the zoo. Some students report returning to the zoo with their own families, and instead of the normal walking around and commenting, "There's a zebra; those are the monkeys," they can share their own, much deeper, understandings of animal behavior.

Margaret's BIG Lesson concept has found eager converts all across the state and has attracted financial support from both public and private agencies. Margaret's own job has evolved; she coordinates the program part-time, helping to find additional sites, offering workshops for teachers, planning BIG Lesson weeks with teachers, and maintaining the Web site. In her "other" life, she has continued as a technology teacher three days a week in her original school.

Testimonials from both students and teachers attest to the value of the BIG Lesson concept. It is an idea that arose directly from the work of teaching, from the "bottom up." It is not the sort of idea that would have emerged from policymakers at the state level or indeed from most principals' offices. To be sure, other individuals and the context helped shape what the project has become, but the energy for it arose from the work of a teacher with an idea.

Looking at Scheduling and Student Assignment

Elm Ridge, an elementary school in Florida, was recognized in the community for the many things it did well: It had a welcoming environment, a challenging curriculum, and high rates of student proficiency on the state tests. But Elena, a teacher at Elm Ridge, became interested in the practice of looping after reading an article and talking with colleagues in other districts. Looping means that an individual teacher stays with a group of students for several years (frequently the first three years), and then "loops back" (on, say, the fourth year) to begin again with a new group.

She could see the advantages: Each teacher comes to know the students deeply and to understand their backgrounds, their interests, their preferences in learning, and their family constellations. There was much less "start-up" time needed at the beginning of the school year to establish the routines and institute new procedures. Furthermore, the students themselves entered each school year knowing one another well and knowing the teacher and his individual style. The few new children who entered the school each year were easily absorbed into the established structure.

Of course, in her conversations, Elena learned of the disadvantages of looping as well: When students stay with a single teacher for three years, any conflicts that occur are magnified; when personalities clash, the effects last much longer than in a traditional arrangement. Elena was still intrigued with the idea and wondered whether it could strengthen the program at Elm Ridge.

As a result of her discussions, and with the encouragement of her principal, Elena posted a notice in the faculty lounge inviting interested teachers to join a study group to investigate the concept of looping and to determine whether it might be effective at their school. Four teachers volunteered for the work, and they arranged a regular time to meet (after school on Thursdays, every other week).

Elena located some articles for the group to read, and the others found material as well. They read and generated questions about possible benefits and challenges to be overcome. The group visited schools in neighboring districts where looping was being practiced to learn from the experience of others and to determine whether they thought it could work in their own school.

After a year of meeting, thinking, and planning, the study group proposed a version of looping for Elm Ridge. They had become convinced of the merits of the approach and were confident that they could overcome the challenges. Elena, with the backup and participation of others in the study group, described the concept to the full faculty and elicited their suggestions and concerns. As a result of that full-faculty discussion of the idea, the plan was slightly modified to the following: Kindergarten on its own, 1st and 2nd grades looped, 3rd grade on its own, and 4th and 5th grades looped. The teachers decided that this configuration would best balance the advantages and disadvantages of looping.

The real work began the next year. With Elena taking the initiative, and with a little time released from their teaching, the primary teachers explored the concept in depth, working out all the practical implications, from classroom assignments, to curriculum articulation, to collaboration on communications with families. The teachers were now truly a team; although each teacher had chief responsibility for working closely with a group of children for two years, they knew they had to work even more closely with each other to ensure consistency across all classes.

In addition, with the help of the principal, the teachers (again, under Elena's leadership) began a series of meetings with the parents of students in the school. The parents needed to be convinced of the merits of the approach, and their apprehensions had to be assuaged. Both the principal and the teachers played an essential role in this process: The teachers were the most knowledgeable about the details of the plan, but the principal was the individual to whom the parents looked for official leadership. After four years, the plan, with a few modifications, was still in place.

What Achievement Gap?

Tom, a high school math teacher in Ohio, noticed an interesting phenomenon in his school. In spite of the school's 18 percent black and Hispanic population, only 5 percent of the students in the advanced math classes were minority students and fewer than a third were female. Furthermore, because of the way the school schedule operated and the fact that the pattern in other disciplines was similar to that in mathematics (although the gender gap was noticeably worse in math), a group of white, mostly affluent students moved from advanced math to AP Biology to Honors English in what was, in effect, a segregated cluster within a supposedly integrated school.

With the encouragement of the principal and 20 minutes of a faculty meeting allocated to him, Tom presented some graphs that described the situation and compared the school's demographic breakdown with the enrollment in advanced classes. As expected, Tom's presentation was greeted with some defensiveness by his colleagues.

But as a result of his invitation, five of his colleagues agreed to participate in a more detailed examination of the situation.

The group explored many aspects of the situation, but the most revealing turned out to be interviews with students and observations of one another's classrooms. They began their discussions by looking at the preparation of different groups of students when they entered from the middle schools. Not surprisingly, they found gaps in achievement in 8th grade among the different groups of students. They might have left it there and determined that the gaps they inherited from the middle schools could not be overcome in high school and that low-performing 8th grade students would be forever relegated to the lower tracks or remedial classes.

To their credit, and partially owing to Tom's polite insistence, the group first did some reading on the role of expectations, on student views of intelligence and ability, and on stereotype threat (Aronson, 2004; Grossman & Ancess, 2004; Landsman, 2004; Sanders & Cotton Nelson, 2004; Steele & Aronson, 1995). They tried to ascertain which of the research findings might offer guidance to the teachers in their efforts to expand minority participation and success in advanced classes. They also learned from their reading (Dweck & Sorich, 1999) that in interactions with students it was essential to praise them less for the products of their work than for their effort. That is, when students believe that by working hard they can do well, they are willing to put forth effort. It is not a matter, in other words, of being good at math or science, but it is a matter of making a sustained effort to master complex material.

While Tom recognized that the approach was risky, he convinced his colleagues that they needed to examine their own practices. Therefore, offering himself as the first subject for study, Tom arranged for his colleagues to interview some of his students and to observe his teaching. The results were stunning. Tom himself was shocked by the findings:

• Many students in his nonhonors math class recalled having been told by a teacher in their early years of schooling that they were not good at math. "And it's true," they would add. "I'm in a low math class."

• When a colleague observed one of Tom's honors math classes, keeping track of the attention he paid to boys and girls, the colleague reported (to Tom's amazement) that even controlling for the different numbers of boys and girls in the class, Tom devoted 80 percent of his time to the boys and only 20 percent to the girls. When Tom made a concerted effort to remedy this pattern and invited the same colleague to observe him again, he learned to his great surprise that his attention was only equally divided, that is, half to the boys and half to the girls. He had predicted that the 80–20 numbers would be reversed; instead, it was exactly 50–50.

• The same observations revealed that Tom's responses to male and female students were markedly different. He gave more time to respond to questions to boys than to girls, and his follow-up questions to boys were significantly deeper and more challenging.

When Tom reported these findings to the other members of the study group, they, too, were surprised and troubled. One by one they agreed to participate in the same sort of research into their own classes. One teacher dropped out of the study group, attributing his action to family commitments. Tom regretted that teacher's decision and hoped that the work of the group had not been too uncomfortable for his colleague. But he was unable to convince him to stay involved.

So with a slightly smaller group, the teachers began to collect information about their own teaching. Again, the results were revealing:

• Minority students who had been in an advanced math class in 9th grade, but did not continue with those classes in later years said that as one of only one or two minority students in their math classes, they felt isolated and unwelcome. They also felt themselves—or believed others regarded them as—imposters, incapable of doing the work and only token members of minority groups.

• Black students in one honors history class reported that the teacher asked the white students the tough questions but directed the easy questions, the ones that "anyone could answer," to the few minority students in the class. When the teacher heard about this comment, she was stunned. She realized the truth of the statement, and said "I just assumed that they didn't know the answer, and I didn't want to embarrass them."

To a greater or lesser extent, all of the teachers involved in the study recognized that they had been operating in denial to some degree; they could quite easily believe that the patterns Tom reported might be a part of other teachers' classrooms, but didn't think that they existed in their own. They acknowledged being upset by what their colleagues had discovered. Tom's role here was interesting. He pointed out to his colleagues that they might have stumbled on some of the factors responsible for the numbers he presented at the original faculty meeting, and that these were clearly under their control. That is, perhaps if teachers did some things differently, the enrollment and achievement patterns in their school could be significantly improved.

Members of the study group went to work, beginning in their own classrooms. They made conscious efforts in their advanced classes to challenge all their students and to monitor their interactions with students of different racial and gender groups. And in their nonhonors classes, they tried to take special care to offer encouragement to their minority and lower-achieving students. Some of the teachers described what they were doing to their students to alert them to the issue and to enlist their help in changing the culture of the classroom.

In weekly meetings of the study group, members reported on these experiences. At first their discussions centered on how difficult it was to confront their own practices. But the environment was safe; they had committed themselves early in the project to honoring one another's efforts and not engaging in one-upmanship or criticism. Even so, the work was difficult.

Gradually, however, they were able to report some successes. These came slowly, of course, but they were real:

• In a class where the teacher had allowed the boys to interrupt the girls, that pattern changed. Interestingly, none of the students had been aware of the problem, but a videotape of the class had made the practice obvious. Once everyone was sensitized to the situation, the boys began to apologize when they interrupted the girls and learned to wait their turn to talk. Just as important, the girls began to stand their ground in class discussions.

• Girls in a physics class had held back during lab work, letting the boys handle the equipment while they kept the data. When the teacher specifically asked the girls to set up an experiment and the boys to record the data, he was confronted with a mutiny. The girls declined to do it: "We don't know how to do it! Can't the boys set it up?" But over time, the teacher was able to shift student perceptions; by the end of the year, the girls were as possessive of the lab equipment as the boys were.

• When the course selections for the next year were announced, the number of girls enrolled in AP physics jumped from 4 of 13 to 10 of 20. That is, both the *absolute* number of girls increased from 5 to 10 and the proportion of the total increased from 31 percent to 50 percent in a single year. By any measure, these are very rapid results.

After several months of these activities, Tom and his colleagues realized that their work was not finished. They asked for a slot on a full-staff meeting agenda to discuss their efforts and their findings with the entire faculty. They also asked for opportunities to share their findings with the middle and elementary school staffs. Eventually, other teachers across the district became interested in the project and began to take steps in their own classrooms. Over time, the results were significant. The participation and achievement rates gradually improved among minority students and, where needed, among girls. But everyone recognized that this issue of participation and achievement gap is a long-term one that would not be fixed overnight. Many teachers also saw implications for how they communicate with families; some students are convinced, sometimes from subtle signals from home, that academic rigor is not a possibility for them. But the project Tom initiated has, over time, had a profound impact on practice.

What Can the Profession Learn from Tom, Margaret, and Elena

By any sensible definition of leadership, Margaret, Elena, and Tom would qualify as leaders. They saw a need; they recognized an opportunity to do something differently for the direct benefit of students; they pulled it off. But their activities don't fit the conceptualizations of school leadership that inform much educational literature.

What, then, is teacher leadership, and how is teacher leadership different from other types of leadership as described in the educational, political, and business literature? Is it a viable and useful concept? It is the premise of this book that the answer to the latter question is a resounding "yes," and that teacher leadership promises to offer a solution to some of the most vexing educational issues we face today. Furthermore, a clearly articulated framework for teacher leadership, one that describes its features and the many ways in which it is demonstrated, may serve to motivate teachers who are seeking to fill a more comprehensive role in their work.

This book explores the work of teacher leaders such as Margaret, Elena, and Tom and places their activities into the broader context of school improvement. It offers guidance for teachers whose gazes are focused on the details of teaching and learning, but who also seek to extend their reach beyond their own classrooms. It provides tips for those administrators who recognize the power of teacher leadership, but are not sure how to cultivate and promote the development of teacher leaders on their own staffs. The premise of this book is that leadership in schools need not be hierarchical;

communication need not be a one-way proposition. And while schools, like other organizations, need to have someone in charge, there are ways of being in charge that not only honor the expertise of teachers but also unleash the power of genuine leadership in them.

2

What Is Teacher Leadership?

The term teacher leadership refers to that set of skills demonstrated by teachers who continue to teach students but also have an influence that extends beyond their own classrooms to others within their own school and elsewhere. It entails mobilizing and energizing others with the goal of improving the school's performance of its critical responsibilities related to teaching and learning. Mobilizing and energizing does not occur because of the role of the leader as boss (as might be the case with a principal), but rather because the individual is informed and persuasive. Therefore, an important characteristic of a teacher leader is expertise and skill in engaging others in complex work. It also entails an unwavering passion for the core mission of the school and the courage to confront obstacles to achieving that mission.

Because improvement of a school's performance frequently involves doing things differently from how they have been done in the past, teacher leadership often requires managing a process of change. But this is not always the case. Many times, improvement occurs when teacher leaders motivate colleagues to become more skilled and thoughtful regarding their work, encouraging them not to do things differently but to do them *better*. At other times, of course, teacher leaders recognize an opportunity to institute a practice that will improve the school's program. In those situations, teacher leadership does require convincing others to use a new approach, but the change process involved is not that of implementing a new program, in which the stages of concern have been well documented (Loucks-Horsley, 1996). Rather, it is a professional exploration of practice.

The popular conception of leadership, whether in the business world, the military, or an educational setting, is that of a lone ranger, a strong individual who works against long odds to accomplish challenging feats. That is not the appropriate image for teacher leaders. Rather, teacher leaders develop a collaborative relationship with colleagues; they inspire others to join them on a journey without a specific destination. They recognize an opportunity or a problem, and they convince others to join them in addressing it. Michael Fullan (2001) put it so well: "The litmus test of all leadership is whether it mobilises people's commitment to putting their energy into actions designed to improve things. It is individual commitment, but above all it is collective mobilisation" (p. 9).

Background to the Concept of Teacher Leadership

Many aspects of teaching distinguish it from other professions, including its relatively low pay and low status, its lack of an apprenticeship period for novices, its oversight by government agencies, and its relatively high degree of union membership. Furthermore, until recently, teaching was one of the few fields (along with nursing) open to educated women. That fact, combined with the bureaucratic nature of schools and the pattern of mostly male administrators supervising mostly female teachers, has reinforced the public perception of teaching as relatively low-skilled work with generous vacations. In fact, in many states and school districts, the work of teaching is regarded as following procedures or instructional plans designed by others and under the close direction of a supervisor. While there are historical reasons for these conditions, it should be noted that they do not prevail in many other countries, where teachers are highly respected and work with a great deal of autonomy. In the United States, however, such characteristics define teaching as semiskilled work in which teachers, at the lowest level of the bureaucratic hierarchy, take direction from their superiors. In recognition of this situation, the educational literature is replete with pleas for teaching to become a true profession.

To be sure, teaching is unique among the professions in the degree of government regulation involved. The state has a vital interest in an educated citizenry; education is a critical factor when it comes to casting a vote and serving on a jury, and an educated workforce is essential to sustained economic development. Furthermore, in most places, students have little choice in the schools they attend or in the teachers in those schools to whom they are assigned. These factors ensure that educators in general, and teachers in particular, are subject to greater state regulation than, say, accountants or architects.

Embedded in the bureaucratic conceptualization of teaching is the fact that teaching is, in most settings, a "flat" profession; the first day on the job for the teacher with 10 years' experience is the same as the first day for a novice just entering the profession. That is, both are the teacher of record, with responsibility for the students in their charge. No architectural firm would ask a newly licensed architect to single-handedly design a major building the first week on the job. Rather, she would work on a team with more experienced architects. Similarly, a newly licensed accountant would not be assigned a major client to handle on his own. At the very least, he would be mentored by an experienced colleague and would gradually assume greater autonomy for the firm's clients.

Clearly, the work of an experienced teacher is not the same as that of a novice. Experience confers many benefits to both educators and their students—familiarity with the curriculum, an understanding of youth, a repertoire of instructional strategies, and deep knowledge of the workings of the school and the district. In other words, experience is frequently (although, it must be admitted, not always) accompanied by expertise. Such expertise results in professional restlessness in some individuals.

Professional restlessness leads to what some teachers have described as a leadership itch: the desire to reach out beyond their own classrooms. In virtually every school and school district, there are teachers who have become skilled in their work with students so that their daily work is not the challenge it was in their first few years. While the profession of teaching is never fully mastered, and while teachers never fully exhaust the potential of their work with students, these individuals seek additional challenges and opportunities to extend their reach. Some teachers want to influence more students than those whom they teach directly each year. Their vision extends beyond their own classrooms and beyond even their own instructional teams or departments. They recognize the school for the complex system it is and see that students' experience in school is a function of more than their interaction with individual teachers; it is influenced by the *systems* in place in the school.

Traditionally, the only ways in which teachers with an inclination for leadership could satisfy their yearnings for greater reach and influence have been either to become administrators or to become active in their teachers unions. For some teachers, depending on the situation and their individual personalities, such career paths are effective. As has been well documented, the role of administrators is critical to a successful school. In addition, in some settings, teachers unions offer opportunities for teachers to exercise leadership within the profession. However, both of these approaches can require leaving the classroom (certainly when going into administration and frequently when actively engaging in a union). By contrast, there are teachers who want to exercise greater influence while continuing their work as a teacher; they feel an urge to exercise leadership as teachers rather than administrators.

Teacher leaders see themselves first as *teachers*; although they are not interested in becoming administrators, they are looking to extend their influence. They are professional educators who want to continue to work as teachers rather than as managers. Some of these skilled teachers enter administration only to return to full-time teaching because they miss the daily interaction with students. Teacher leaders are more than teachers, yet different from administrators. Such a concept of teacher leadership reflects an increasingly recognized hole in models of teacher professionalism that has not yet been fully explored in the professional literature.

The concept of teacher leadership also recognizes that teachers' tenure in a school is normally longer than that of the administrators who are nominally in charge (20–30 years for many teachers as compared with the typical 3–5 years for a principal). The school change and leadership literature is replete with examples of schools that have been turned around by an inspired, and inspiring, principal but that have then reverted to their previous state when that individual moved to another position. Therefore, the cultivation of teacher leadership may well be a wise investment for a school district committed to improving practice over the long term. It may also prove decisive in encouraging gifted teachers to remain with education rather than abandon the profession for one that offers greater opportunities for ongoing challenge and advancement.

Furthermore, in most schools, traditional norms of autonomy and individuality work against the development of professional learning communities, which are essential for meaningful school improvement. That is, it is increasingly recognized that if schools are to achieve better results with their students, it must be a collective endeavor rather than a collection of individual efforts. Teacher leadership, when exercised by educators respected by their colleagues, makes a significant contribution to de-privatizing practice —so critical for collective learning.

The concept of teacher leadership did not spring into being in the early years of the 21st century. Rather, it has a long history in various forms, reaching back for more than 100 years. However, while the concept of teacher leadership is not new, it has been featured prominently in the literature of school reform and improvement, particularly in light of its connection to broader school reform efforts. As with much else in U.S. education, the antecedents of our current thinking about teacher leadership rest with John Dewey. An important part of Dewey's advocacy of the democratic society was his insistence on democratic schools. This vision included both students and teachers as partners in the democratic venture. Throughout the 20th century, enlightened school boards and administrators recognized that if teachers were to embrace the school's policies and organizational structures, they had to be part of the processes that created them. Hence, many schools created site councils to make decisions affecting the school; teachers have traditionally played an important role on those bodies. These arrangements were in direct response to the notion, best stated by John Dewey (1903), that it was essential that "every teacher had some regular and representative way to register judgment upon matters of educational importance, with assurance that this judgment would somehow affect the school system" (p. 195). In 1986, the Carnegie Forum on Education and the Economy concluded that teachers should have "more control over their work environments" (p. 103). Thus, the concept of teacher participation in school decision making has a long history, with teachers involved in school governance. However, teacher participation in school governance, as important as it is, hinges on the assumption that the principal responsibility for school governance rests with administrators. That is, teachers, rather than taking initiative for what happens in the school, are invited to participate in making decisions. True teacher leadership, as conceptualized in this book, involves spontaneous and organic teacher initiative and facilitation, ideas absent from earlier work in the field.

Connections to Related Concepts

The concept of teacher leadership rests within a web of concepts regarding leadership in educational and organizational settings and is best understood in relation to these other ideas.

Leadership as Administration

In educational circles, the term school leader means the site administrator; university programs for school leaders prepare principals and superintendents for their roles.

The professional literature in educational leadership focuses almost exclusively on the role of the principal, with excursions into the leadership exercised by central office administrators such as superintendents, assistant superintendents, staff developers, and curriculum directors.

The Interstate School Leaders Licensing Consortium (ISLLC), an outgrowth of the Council of Chief State School Officers, has defined school leadership (taken to mean administrative leadership) as consisting of six standards, all intended to support the principal's essential responsibility as instructional leader. These standards, which have been adopted by many states as criteria for the licensing of administrators, may be summarized as establishing and maintaining a vision; providing instructional leadership (in all its manifestations); managing the building; interacting with the broader community; maintaining high ethical standards; and interacting with the larger political, social, economic, and cultural context. For each of these standards, the document *Standards for School Leaders* (Council of Chief State School Officers, 1996) describes knowledge, dispositions, and performances that, taken together, serve to further define each standard. According to this approach, it is not sufficient for school administrators to be good managers; they must be visionary educational leaders who can mobilize and inspire their school communities in the service of high-level student learning. Hence, ISLLC's definition of leadership, while focused on the role of administrators, does not rest solely, or even mainly, on the administrators as managers; they must also be instructional leaders. Nonetheless, they are undeniably administrators.

Administrative leadership is essential to successful schools. Since the effective schools research of the 1970s, strong administrative leadership has been recognized as critical to high levels of student learning (Waters, Marzano, & McNulty, 2003). More recently, a study of urban school districts has reaffirmed the importance of the principal's role in promoting high levels of achievement (Simmons, 2004). Although it may be a necessary condition for school improvement, administrative leadership is not sufficient; it must be complemented by teacher leadership, that informal, spontaneous exercise of initiative and creativity that results in enhanced student learning. The litmus test of effective leadership (exercised by administrators or teachers) is whether improved learning survives the departure of the leader, whether it has become institutionalized.

Sustainability goes even further. Sustainability, as described by Andy Hargreaves (in press), is the institutionalization not of changed practice but of the *habit* of critically examining practice. Embedding these habits of mind into the daily work of schools cannot happen without leadership, and it is part of the leadership exercised by administrators. Therefore, the concept of teacher leadership is neither in conflict nor in competition with the idea of administrative leadership. They are complementary concepts that ideally work together on behalf of students and their learning.

Leadership as Management of Change

Some writers, notably Michael Fullan (2001), have conceptualized leadership as the management of change, often large-scale change. Such efforts require leadership skills, to be sure; the history of education is littered with the corpses of innovations that did not survive the departure of a heroic leader. Managing change, therefore, requires not only initiating but also institutionalizing and sustaining changed practice. Furthermore, large-scale change—affecting a school district or indeed an entire state or country—is frequently accompanied by revisions in policy and is typically supported by a large infusion of resources.

But teacher leadership rarely involves large-scale, systemic change. Changed practice that results from teacher leadership is significant and can reach into the very crevices of a school's program. But it is very different from the large-scale implementation of new programs that is typically involved in systemic change. Although the literature on leadership as management of change is important to our understanding of leadership in general, it does not fully explain the concept of teacher leadership as described here.

Formal Teacher Leadership Roles

Many schools have instituted structures in which teachers assume formal leadership roles in the school, such as master teacher, department chair, team leader, helping teacher, or mentor. These arrangements recognize the essential role of teachers as key players in the broader effort toward enhanced student achievement. Such roles are not created to engage teachers primarily in establishing schools as democratic societies. Rather, they are created to distribute the work of running schools to others besides the principal and to enlist teachers as partners in school improvement.

Such role-based positions do represent opportunities for leadership by teachers. And while the term distributed leadership has been used in a number of different senses, it frequently connotes such spreading, or "stretching"—to use Spillane, Halverson, and Diamond's (2001) vivid term—of responsibility among different individuals in the organization. However, to the extent that teachers are placed in roles of influence and decision making, other teachers may regard them as quasi-administrators. This is particularly the case if teachers must apply for the position and be selected and if the role carries supervisory responsibilities. Even when teachers in formal roles play no part in the evaluation process, some teachers regard those who are "appointed and anointed" to such positions as breaking ranks with the solidarity of teachers, as no longer being true colleagues. In other words, they may be seen as administrators in teachers' clothing. Furthermore, depending on the selection criteria and process used, those appointed to leadership positions may or may not possess real leadership skills; at the worst, the entire endeavor may smack of favoritism, with the credibility of the entire enterprise undermined. Teachers in formal or semiformal roles are more likely to be trusted by other teachers when the members of the instructional team or the department elect their leader and when the roles rotate each year.

A variation on the theme of teacher as quasi-administrator is the concept of "teacher on special assignment." Such an arrangement typically enables a teacher (usually selected by the administrator) to serve as the coordinator for implementing a new program or to assist colleagues with a new approach or strategy. The assignment recognizes that teachers may be the true experts in the field and that they cannot serve as resources to their colleagues while teaching full-time. Teachers who hold these positions, particularly when the positions are temporary—as they generally are—are rarely regarded as pseudo-administrators.

When teachers who serve in formal leadership roles remain teachers in the eyes of their colleagues, the concepts of shared decision making or distributed leadership are still of limited value in understanding teacher leadership. They suggest that someone—typically an administrator—is doing the sharing of decision making or the distributing of leadership. This implies that those decisions and that leadership are the administrator's to share or distribute; in other words, these positions are an extension of administrative leadership.

Teacher leadership, by contrast, is spontaneously exercised by teachers (any teacher) in response to a need or an opportunity through work with colleagues. It emerges organically; no one appoints teacher leaders to their roles. And while administrators may (and usually do) play an important supporting role, the initiative comes from the teacher.

Why Teacher Leadership?

As stated earlier, interest in teacher leadership has increased substantially in recent years. Why is this? Why are educators and policymakers suddenly interested in this phenomenon?

The Managerial Imperative

Educational leadership, as described in the professional literature and typically referring to administrative leadership at the school site, has become a gigantic task, beyond the capacity of any but the most capable and energetic principal. Richard Elmore describes it well:

> Reading the literature on the principalship can be overwhelming, because it suggests that principals should embody all the traits and skills that remedy all the defects of the schools in which they work. They should be in close touch with their communities, inside and outside the school; they should, above all, be masters of human relations, attending to all the conflicts and disagreements that might arise among students, among teachers, and among anyone else who chooses to create a conflict in the school; they should be both respectful of the authority of district administrators and crafty at deflecting administrative intrusions that disrupt the autonomy of teachers; they should keep an orderly school; and so on. Somewhere on the list one usually finds a reference to instruction. (2000, p. 14)

The vast literature (and it is vast) on school leadership has defined the principal variously as requiring some or all of the following forms of leadership: technical, professional, transactional, and transformational. Other models of leadership focus on its political, managerial, or cultural dimensions. When distilled, these concepts all seek to establish the principal as the inspirational head of the complex organization called school. The principal is to shepherd the school toward the achievement of demanding imperatives mandated by national, state, and district policy. The sheer range of the descriptions of what the principal's work encompasses attests to the size and complexity of the role.

Not surprisingly, school administrators are staggering under the load; human resources personnel report that principalships are increasingly difficult to fill. As instructional leaders and as managers, site administrators are burdened with huge responsibilities under increasing pressure from their own districts and government agencies and with student populations that are increasingly diverse in academic and social preparation and in English language skills. A principal in New York City has reported that the legal mandates he received from the superintendent's office in a single year weighed in at 45 pounds (Howard, 2004). The job has become virtually impossible to do well. Small wonder, then, that thoughtful educators increasingly recognize that administrators, in order to discharge their responsibilities, must cultivate a culture of inquiry and responsibility for student learning among their faculties. They must, in other words, cultivate teacher leaders. As Elmore (2000) describes it,

> the job of administrative leaders is primarily about enhancing the skills and knowledge of people in the organization, creating a common culture of expectations around the use of those skills and knowledge, holding the various pieces of the organization together in a productive relationship with each other, and holding individuals accountable for their contribution to the collective results (p. 15).

The School Improvement Imperative

Schools are under unrelenting pressure to improve results for all students, with a particular focus on those students previously underserved. That is, schools must at least make progress toward closing the achievement gap among different groups of students. Of course, a political agenda drives some of the initiatives (from both federal and state agencies), but thoughtful educators support at least the aims of the legislation and regulations, if not the details of implementation. In any event, schools are the locus of accountability; the school can be shut down if it does not show adequate results.

Principals are the technical leaders of schools, and the buck stops with them. They recognize, however, that they cannot improve schools by themselves. There is increasing recognition in both the academic and the practitioner literature that even if principals wanted to be the sole leaders of their schools, they could not meet the standards now being set for them. As Katzenmeyer and Moller (2001) put it, "When given opportunities to lead, teachers can influence school reform efforts. Waking this sleeping giant of teacher leadership has unlimited potential in making a real difference in the pace and depth of school change" (p. 102).

Professionalization of Teaching

It is generally accepted that the most important factor contributing to student learning is the quality of teaching, supported by other components in the school's organization such as the curriculum, the programs and policies for students, and the nature of connections with the external community. And with increasing external pressures for high-level and universal student achievement, many educators recognize that administrators alone do not effect that achievement. Even if they want to maintain a traditional and hierarchical structure, administrators must find ways to unleash the expertise of the teachers on their staffs and to capture the energy and knowledge of those who know the most about what works in the classroom.

Traditional views of leadership as residing exclusively in administrative positions portray teachers as immature beings (children, almost) who need direction and guidance. Some definitions of teaching regard important curriculum design decisions as better left to experts, with teachers implementing others' designs. By contrast, the view of teaching that underlies the concept of teacher leadership sees teaching as professional work in which teachers are informed by professional research and make complex decisions and exercise judgment and autonomy in support of student learning. Teaching requires complex decision making, frequently under conditions of uncertainty and high levels of pressure. Therefore, the role of leadership in a school setting, whether exercised by teachers or administrators, involves supporting the decision making of teachers in the service of student learning.

Related to the professional nature of teaching is the concept of expertise and where it resides. In any bureaucratic structure in which one group of individuals (administrators) exercises supervisory control over another (teachers), it is assumed that those with authority also have the greater expertise. That is, if the principal's role is seen to be that of improving instruction, it is assumed that the principal is more of an expert on teaching than are the teachers. This may not be the case. It is virtually impossible for an administrator of a secondary school to be knowledgeable about all the subjects taught there and their accompanying pedagogy. Similarly, primary teachers may be more expert in the area of early childhood learning and development than the administrators who supervise their work. The concept of teacher leadership, while acknowledging the essential role of administrators in ensuring at least a minimum quality of teaching and supporting its continuing improvement, also recognizes that the expertise in a school, in both the content and in the methods of instruction, rests with teachers. The concept also reshapes the role of site administrator to that of facilitator of learning for both teachers and students.

Thus, the idea of teacher leadership stems from a conceptualization of teaching as complex work requiring expertise, judgment, and a high degree of autonomy (informed by a knowledge of the professional literature). Teacher leadership is exercised in the equally complex environment of schools, school districts, and government agencies. Small wonder that it is a concept that has not been fully described or elaborated.

Issues Involved in Teacher Leadership

Some educators may fear that teacher leadership would be difficult to bring to life in their own setting. Indeed, there are issues that could present obstacles to fully enabling teacher leaders to emerge. These issues are discussed in the following sections.

Contested Ground

Little (1995) and, later, Lieberman and Miller (2004) describe the "contested ground" between teachers and administrators. Some administrators are reluctant to cede what they consider their authority to teachers, and they don't provide sufficient opportunities for teachers to work together and exercise leadership responsibilities. Granted, this research was conducted primarily within the context of appointed leaders (for example, department chairs), but the concern is also real in a more informal definition of teacher leadership presented here.

The issue is more than one of time for teachers to work together; it is about power. Principals play an essential role in effective schools. Teachers know that. They know that they can obtain their best results with students only in a school that is well managed under the guidance of a strong instructional leader. But principals, when recognizing and cultivating teacher leadership, enhance their own standing within the school. It is one of the surprising features of leadership that in sharing power, one increases one's authority. This issue will be addressed more fully in Chapter 8.

Negotiated Agreements

In some school districts, contracts negotiated with teachers unions include specific guidelines regarding what teachers may and may not be asked to do in the school. Virtually all contracts specify the number of contact minutes teachers have with students. But others also specify that teachers will be compensated for any time they spend on school matters beyond student contact hours. This typically includes such things as helping out in the lunchroom or the playground and may extend to other matters, such as supervising student activities and clubs. Such provisions may make it difficult for teachers to take on projects on their own initiative. It is not the purpose of this book to undermine either the letter or the spirit of negotiated agreements; their provisions prevent teachers from being exploited and have done a great deal for the profession. At the same time, however, it would be regrettable if these agreements became obstacles to the professionalism of teaching and the efforts of gifted teachers to exercise leadership. In some situations the unions have taken the lead, offering opportunities to their members to acquire leadership skills and to take on projects requiring initiative and support. The recognition that such teachers receive serves to strengthen the profession.

State Requirements

In virtually every state, teachers no longer receive a permanent license to teach; rather, a license is granted for a fixed term (for example, five years) and is renewable on demonstration of a certain amount of professional development, typically counted in "hours." And in some school districts, teachers are eligible for movement on the salary schedule based on their work in school and district projects. The activities of teacher leaders could be accommodated by these arrangements; it is conceivable that a teacher leader's project could satisfy state or district requirements or be sufficient to result in movement on the salary schedule.

Teacher Leadership Versus Formal Roles

Teacher leaders can emerge in many different ways. Occasionally, an external mandate imposes a new requirement on schools, such as extensive teacher and student use of computers, and a teacher proposes an innovative way to address the mandate (Lieberman & Miller, 2004). In such cases, the teacher leader is opportunistic, using the mandate (and sometimes the funding that accompanies it) as an excuse to mobilize colleagues and pursue important work. In other situations, the initiative is one that simply arises from a perceived need, without the push from external factors.

In either type of situation, what began as a spontaneous exercise of teacher leadership may metamorphose into a more formal role. Margaret's BIG Lessons (from Chapter 1) did just that. Her project began as something she did in her school in which colleagues became interested. However, in the ensuing years, with recognition and funding from state agencies, it has become a formal responsibility three days a week. She continues to teach, but she is also project director of the BIG Lesson concept in Michigan. Similarly, a state initiative for increased technology use was mandated by Maine in 2001. It attracted a teacher who saw a way to implement the initiative in a manner clearly superior to that proposed by the state agency. When it was recognized as such, the state contracted with her to coordinate the statewide effort. In these instances, the teacher leaders did not remain full-time teachers; at least temporarily, their responsibilities changed.

The Relationship with Accomplished Teaching

Some educators argue that teacher leaders have already been identified and recognized through certification by the National Board for Professional Teaching Standards. It is true that the National Board process is rigorous and very worthwhile, and that one of the portfolio entries does touch on teacher leadership. But in the main, teachers earn National Board certification by demonstrating their excellence in the classroom, by reflecting thoughtfully on their practice, and by demonstrating deep knowledge of their subjects, their students, and the principles of instructional design.

It is important that teachers who aspire to leadership roles within their school have demonstrated excellence in teaching and been recognized as skilled by their colleagues. This provides critical credibility. That is, a teacher's first responsibility is to her own students; it is only when teaching performance is at (or above) standard that teachers can truly assume leadership roles. Furthermore, other teachers are far more likely to join an effort with a colleague if that teacher is respected in the school as an exemplary teacher.

How Teacher Leadership Is Demonstrated

Teacher leadership may be exercised in any area of school life. This framework for teacher leadership is divided into three areas: schoolwide policies and programs, teaching and learning, and communications and community relations. Each area contains three or four smaller areas, as illustrated in Figure 2.1. For example, Margaret's concept of the BIG Lesson initially involved a different relationship with a community agency (the museum) that later affected instructional practice. Tom's interest in differential participation rates by different groups of students focused initially on instructional practice but had implications for student assignment to classes. And Elena's looping project squarely concerned the school's organizational structure.

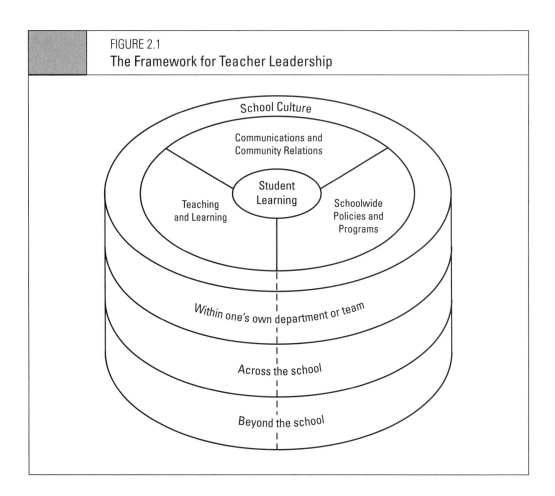

FIGURE 2.1
The Framework for Teacher Leadership

Furthermore, teacher leadership is exhibited in any number of settings in the school: within one's own instructional team or department, throughout the school, or beyond the school in the district, the state, or even the entire nation. For example, Tom's effort in his high school was conducted primarily within the math department, although it spread to the entire school and beyond. Elena's efforts in looping affected the entire school (or at least half the school—the primary teachers) right from the outset. Margaret's BIG Lesson began as a project in her own class but has now spread across the state. Teacher leaders who operate at the state and national level are the voice of teachers on state policy boards or on broader curriculum committees.

None of these settings is to be preferred over any other; they are simply different locations of work. Furthermore, it is sometimes more of a challenge to convince one's close colleagues to attempt a new approach than it is to promote something on a state or even national level; a department or team is more like family and may be more critical of one's ideas. These settings, together with the areas of school life in which teacher leadership might be demonstrated, are summarized in Figure 2.1. In Part II of this book, examples of teacher leadership activities in each of the three settings will be provided for each area of school life.

The concept of teacher leadership recognizes the daunting challenges confronting schools of the 21st century and the need for schools, as organizations, to meet those challenges through innovative structures. Clearly, the strict bureaucratic hierarchy is not sufficient, nor are other approaches that place teachers in the role of receiver of accepted wisdom. Rather, to bring the best to bear on the challenges of education, the engagement of teacher leaders in the enterprise is an important component of any improvement strategy.

Teacher leadership is an idea whose time has definitely arrived. The profession, through the work of the National Board for Professional Teaching Standards, has identified the characteristics of accomplished teachers and has devised methods for recognizing that level of performance. In addition, educators have identified the components of skilled administrative leadership. The time has come to render the same service for those teachers who choose to remain primarily teachers of students, but who have the inclination and the skill to extend their reach. The framework for teacher leadership represents a movement in that direction.

3

What Do Teacher Leaders Do?

As described in the previous chapter, teacher leaders work as teachers but exercise leadership with their colleagues in improving student learning in their schools. (For a comprehensive description of the activities of teacher leaders, see Collinson, 2004.) It is an important concept; teacher leaders play a critical role in improvement efforts and demonstrate an enhanced sense of professionalism. For teachers to become teacher leaders, and for administrators to promote the development of teacher leaders within their schools, it is essential to describe in greater specificity exactly what it is that teacher leaders do and how they do it. In other words, what are the patterns of behavior that Margaret, Tom, and Elena demonstrated in exercising leadership in their schools?

The characteristics of teacher leaders are divided into two major categories: skills and dispositions. Taken together, these are at the heart of what is meant by teacher leadership. Furthermore, there are important and complex relationships between teacher leadership and administrative leadership; neither can exist without the other.

Leadership Skills

Teacher leadership comprises a number of specific skills. And while not every act of leadership includes all the skills, all acts require most skills, and in roughly the sequence presented here.

Using Evidence and Data in Decision Making

Decisions about what to do in schools are not based on feelings and hunches. Rather, they are grounded in evidence that actions will serve to accomplish a particular purpose. Therefore, when teacher leaders see an opportunity, when they identify a need, their focus on the area is based on evidence. This evidence need not be a single set of discrete data; it may result from informal, although systematic, observation. And it may not depend on hard data at all; it may reflect informal patterns observed (and possibly even documented) over a long period.

For example, Tom's interest was piqued by the data regarding differential participation and achievement rates among different subpopulations of the high school in advanced courses. He recognized that if the school was to honor its commitment to educate all students to high levels, such patterns had to be broken. But the first step in changing the pattern was to understand it; for this, the observation of classes (including his own) and the interviews with students were absolutely critical. And when he and his colleagues made some changes and achieved results, those results were captured in data, both hard data regarding enrollment and anecdotal data regarding student willingness to participate in discussions and to take risks in class.

Margaret noticed that her students were not fully engaged in the museum's exhibits; she saw that they preferred milling about in the gift shop over learning from the docents. Her evidence in this case was her observation of student conduct. Elena, on the other hand, was persuaded by the research literature on student grouping and achievement as a consequence of the relationships between teacher and students. In addition, through conversations with educators in other schools using the looping model, she learned of the results that came from practicing the approach.

Other teacher leaders might be motivated in their choice of areas to improve by an observation (frequently supplemented by the comments and complaints of other teachers) that students are seriously deficient in an important aspect of their learning, such as writing. They may have determined, and may have been told by teachers from the next grade or level, that students' writing is unclear, poorly organized, and weak in its use of language.

Teacher leaders do not interpret evidence and data narrowly; they fully understand the limitations of standardized tests. Although test results can, at times, point to a weakness in a school's program, there are many other sources of evidence of both problems and indications of progress that can be used. These include attendance rates;

enrollment patterns in advanced courses; discipline referrals; student work; and survey or focus group data from students, teachers, or parents. Teacher leaders, while recognizing the need for evidence, are flexible and creative in their use of that data.

Recognizing an Opportunity and Taking Initiative

A critical characteristic of leadership is the ability to take initiative. When asked for examples of teachers who have demonstrated leadership, educators consistently cite individuals who have taken initiative in addressing a problem or in improving the school's instructional program.

All three teachers discussed in Chapter 1 demonstrated this characteristic. Margaret was troubled by student engagement, or lack of it, in the museum's offerings. But she did not simply wring her hands or complain to her colleagues. Instead, she thought it through. She set up a meeting with the museum staff to explore options. She discussed the idea with her principal. In other words, she took initiative. So did Elena. Elena was motivated less by a problem than by an opportunity to improve. That is, the previous method of assigning students to teachers was not causing difficulty; the school could have continued it with no ill effects. But Elena saw what she thought might be an opportunity for improvement and initiated a focused examination of looping. And Tom, as a result of examining the data, initiated a project to look beneath the data to try to understand the causes for the numbers.

An important aspect of taking initiative consists of looking around and being alert to opportunities for improvement; in that sense, it is the opposite of complacency. Teacher leaders are never content with the status quo, recognizing that no matter how successful a school is, it could always be at least a little bit better. So the skill of taking initiative is coupled with an ongoing quest for, and commitment to, improvement.

Mobilizing People Around a Common Purpose

A teacher leader is able to describe a vision for a better future and can communicate it clearly and persuasively enough to colleagues to help them both see its potential and join in the effort. A teacher leader does not simply see an opportunity and take initiative to address it all alone. Instead, he engages others in the project. Furthermore, the approach is invitational, perhaps taking the form of, "I've been noticing that _____, and I wonder whether _____ couldn't help us address it. What do you think? Do you agree that it is a problem? Do you think that might work? Or is there a better approach?"

Again, all three teachers involved others in their approach. But it should also be recognized that they all had done some preliminary reading and thinking. Elena made herself familiar with the workings of looping before she mobilized her colleagues to examine it more deeply. Margaret had preliminary conversations with the museum staff before she developed the idea of the BIG Lesson sufficiently to describe it to other teachers. And Tom summarized the enrollment data before he made his initial presentation to the full faculty. In all three cases, the concept as implemented was somewhat different from (and presumably better than) the original idea. In Tom's case, the initial effort was to collect information and gain an understanding of the factors that were contributing to the findings. In all cases, the projects took on lives of their own, shaped by their originators but also influenced by the perspectives of others. The vision remained constant—that is the role of the leader—but the details of action resulted from collegial conversation and deliberation.

In addition, at the stage when Margaret's and Elena's ideas were to be put into action, the parents of the students involved had to be convinced of the merits of the plan. This is an important communication requirement, and one for which they both needed and took advantage of the principal's essential role as the official voice of the school to the outside world. In addition to fostering parent understanding of and support for the plan, communicating the idea to parents is an important step in refining the plan itself. In the course of the discussion, parents may have suggestions to strengthen the approach.

Marshaling Resources and Taking Action

At some point, it is time to take action, to try something. This "something" can range from embarking on a large-scale new project to approaching a business to ask for lab equipment. In the end, talking about doing something is not sufficient. Teacher leaders can do their homework, they can talk to colleagues, and they can conduct research, but they may have to simply commit to a course of action without fully knowing its consequences. At some point in the planning and implementation of a project, it is essential to make a commitment to action. In other words, talking can go on only so long before people become restive at the lack of real action. Teacher leaders provide the energy for that action; they are the individuals who, at the appropriate point, are willing to roll up their sleeves and just do it.

It is a reality of school life that resources are sometimes needed, such as funds to pay for conference fees, an outside consultant, or substitute teachers, to provide teachers with the opportunity to meet. These resources may be assembled from school funds or from outside the school; in either case, they need to be garnered. The teacher leader may be the one who will take the initiative in obtaining resources, although frequently the assistance of the site administrator is needed.

To try her idea of a weeklong museum study trip, Margaret needed buses for five days' travel to the museum, rather than the one day typically allocated per class. She also hoped to enlist volunteer help during each of the days, and her lesson plans required some additional materials and supplies. All in all, she required additional resources to implement the extended study lesson, and she solicited them, with the help of her principal, from "downtown," from the parents of her students, and from the museum itself. In later years, as the project spread to other schools and communities, she was able to obtain support from the state government and from a foundation grant.

Elena's initial requirements were more modest. She did the initial exploration of looping on her own, but when she attracted the interest of colleagues, they appealed to the principal for funds to be used to purchase some books and articles, to give teachers time to hold extended planning meetings, and to visit schools where the practice was in use. These needed resources were not enormous, but neither were they negligible. When it came time to implement the looping plan, the teachers discovered that they needed professional development to be effective with students in grade levels different from those they had been teaching. That is, when the 1st grade teacher moved with her class to 2nd grade, or when the 4th grade teacher moved with her class to the 5th grade, she had work to do in learning the curricula and the teaching methods for older students.

In Tom's case, also, the resources needed initially were modest and primarily consisted of substitutes who could relieve the members of the study group from a small portion of their classroom responsibilities so they could meet together and observe one another's classrooms. But the interview questions for students, the observation protocols, and the subsequent data analysis were strengthened by the participation of an evaluation expert paid for by school funds. In addition, for the research reading portion of the project, the teachers wanted to purchase a few books and locate relevant articles for discussion.

Monitoring Progress and Adjusting the Approach as Conditions Change

Teacher leaders are alert to changing conditions and unexpected outcomes. In other words, they recognize that nothing is ever finished; everything is subject to revision and improvement. This applies to almost any sphere of school life in which a teacher leader would operate, from a new program for students, to an approach to professional development for colleagues, to a partnership with the business community.

Monitoring of progress is accompanied by skill in reflection. Teacher leaders engage in critical reflection on the consequences of actions, on the impact of an approach on student learning. The power of reflection on the practice of teaching has been well documented (Kolb, 1984), and teacher leaders engage in critical reflection on their own teaching. They extend this habit of mind to other projects with which they are involved, ensuring that difficulties are recognized and adjustments are made as the work progresses.

Margaret's BIG Lesson concept has been evolving since its inception. It has expanded significantly to include five locations, and teachers and institutions all over the state are now involved. In addition, the Internet has become a significant resource for the project, since it enables teachers to share ideas with one another and precludes the need for teachers to develop every lesson from scratch. Other teachers have contributed their own ideas as to where to take the concept of the BIG Lesson, exploring collaborations with organizations in their own communities.

The looping concept, as implemented, represented a modification of the models the study group examined; that is, none of the schools they visited or read about had an approach that Elena's group thought would fit perfectly at Elm Ridge. And even as they were engaged in their detailed planning year, the teachers discovered that some of their initial plans had to be altered.

Tom's examination of the achievement gap was always expected to evolve as the members of the study group learned more. The project was established as an exploration—initially an exploration of the causes of the gaps in participation and achievement, which was later extended to an exploration of the teachers' own practices that might contribute to such gaps. Once some of these factors were identified, the shape and direction of the project changed accordingly. And, as Tom and his colleagues would fully admit, the project is not finished; indeed, there is probably no such thing as "finished" in such an effort.

Adjusting the approach does not always mean making minor changes. It is conceivable that as a project moves forward, the participants may recognize that the entire approach is misguided. That is, the adjustment could take the form of subjecting it to a major overhaul or even abandoning the effort.

Sustaining the Commitment of Others and Anticipating Negativity

Teacher leadership involves, of course, enlisting the interest and support of colleagues in an identified area. But getting people involved is not sufficient; they need to stay involved. Many projects run into the sand when the initial flush is over, and people and behaviors return to their old patterns.

Sustaining the commitment of others involves skills of facilitation and group process, such as listening, joint problem solving, honoring other people's ideas, maintaining focus, and knowing when to move forward. Teacher leaders are able to be clear about purpose and to remind colleagues of that purpose when needed, while conveying a genuine respect for the concerns and contributions of colleagues. In addition, they are not derailed by colleagues who choose not to become involved or who plant seeds of doubt with others to subtly undermine the effort.

All three teachers in our stories exercised skill and perseverance in maintaining the commitment of others as their projects moved forward. Margaret had to maintain her focus on the goal of richer contacts with the museum; it would have been easy and perhaps tempting to revert to a traditional field trip approach. But in her discussions with the museum staff, in her negotiations with her principal and district officials, and in her explanations of the approach to colleagues and parents of students in her class, Margaret demonstrated clarity of vision and persuasiveness in keeping others on board. To be sure, she adjusted the approach based on others' thoughts and contributions, but her role in keeping people involved was vital.

Elena's leadership in maintaining others' commitment to looping was also essential. She had a vision and guided her colleagues to examine it closely. At the critical stage of making the concept a reality, she kept the energy level high and persuaded others to take on parts of the detailed planning, such as room allocation, materials, training, and parent meetings, that were needed to bring the concept to fruition.

In Tom's case, the need to maintain others' commitment was imperative, and indeed, he was not fully successful in that one teacher dropped out of the study group. But it could also be argued that convincing teachers to examine their practices deeply is more threatening than redesigning field trips as study trips. In any event, as Tom's study group moved forward in its work, and as teachers began to identify factors that contributed to the issue he had raised, Tom played a significant role in sustaining their commitment to the project. It became easier as time went on, particularly as the teachers began to see positive results from their efforts.

It is important to recognize that it is at this stage that many worthwhile projects falter. Teachers, after all, have important and time-consuming work in their own classrooms; in the popular vernacular, they already have day jobs. When a teacher leader approaches colleagues to become involved in an additional effort, it is just that: additional. Not all teachers, particularly those new to the profession, can take it on, even when someone else is providing the leadership. Convincing others to spend time on such a project and sustaining that commitment requires skills of persuasion and clarity of vision: in other words, leadership.

Contributing to a Learning Organization

It is not only individuals who learn, but organizations. As teachers in a school improve their practice and share their findings with colleagues, the collective wisdom increases. Furthermore, as more teachers are engaged in the pursuit of improved practice, the school itself becomes increasingly defined as an organization that learns. Of course, innovative practice is worth doing even when it is carried out by a single individual. However, it is only when shared that improved practice and the habit of improving practice can become institutionalized into the life of the school, or even more broadly. Teacher leaders make an active contribution to the school's collective wisdom not through bragging or attracting attention, but by sharing findings and extending the application of new practices.

Again, all three teachers have made significant contributions to their own schools and, more broadly, to the profession. Margaret's BIG Lesson concept is used all over Michigan, and educators everywhere can log onto the Web site to receive inspiration and perhaps ideas for their own planning. In Elena's case, looping has now become one of the local models. Not only have all the teachers in her school seen the benefits and a few drawbacks to the approach, but the school now hosts visits from educators from other schools who are investigating the practice for possible implementation in their own settings. And Tom's group, by presenting their approach and findings to the school's faculty and to the faculties of other schools in the district, has made a substantial contribution to the collective understanding of all the district's educators.

Teacher leaders may also contribute to the collective wisdom of the profession through outreach to educators at other schools or presentations at state and local conferences. They recognize that the true benefits of improved practice are not realized when confined to a single setting; they must become incorporated into the more general professional community.

Dispositions

Dispositions largely define an individual's approach to situations; when we think about a person, we recall less about that person's skills or even interests than we do about their traits such as optimism and energy. Teacher leaders possess certain dispositions that influence their work with both students and colleagues. These dispositions share some characteristics with, but are not the same as, the habits of mind described by Art Costa and Bena Kallick (2000). Teacher leaders are "can do" people; they do not adopt a defeatist attitude when things go poorly. Instead, when the going gets tough, they get busy. But they don't forge ahead blindly; they weigh options, consider alternatives, and assemble colleagues to help solve problems.

So what are the dispositions that tend to define teacher leaders? This list does not purport to be comprehensive, but it provides a sense of the personalities of those teachers who emerge to lead their colleagues in important initiatives.

Deep Commitment to Student Learning

First of all, teacher leaders have an essential focus on the core mission of enhancing student learning. They never lose sight of that purpose, even when such a focus requires bucking the system or pointing out to colleagues that a proposed approach or an existing practice will undermine learning for some students.

It is not sufficient to espouse, as many educators do, that "all children can learn" and then continue to live and work in schools where many students are not learning or at least are not learning to their potential or even close to it. Teacher leaders know that this is not an acceptable situation, and they focus their energies on changing it. No matter what project they take on, these teachers recognize that the scale by which the school and the efforts of the educators within it is measured is the extent to which it is able to promote high-level learning on the part of all students.

Optimism and Enthusiasm

Attempting new approaches or seeking better ways to achieve previous goals implies that a person believes that better results are possible. The teacher leader is not resigned to business as usual with less than optimal results. Instead, the actions of a teacher leader are driven by optimism and the belief that any situation can be improved.

Teacher leaders tend to look on the bright side of things. They hold high expectations for themselves and expect the best of others. When interpreting others' actions or statements, they tend to ascribe positive motives. This carries a danger, of course, of naiveté; it is possible to be sucked in by the words and promises of others. But the consequence of always doubting the motives of others is worse: it is cynicism. Teacher leaders, by taking an optimistic view of life, tend to steer events in a positive direction.

A characteristic that sets some people apart from others and can be highly motivational to colleagues is enthusiasm. An attitude of "Let's try it!" can infuse energy into an otherwise dispirited group of educators. This attitude is not, it should be clear, a matter of immature exuberance, where action is unrestrained by thought or planning. Instead, it represents energy to pursue a project with vigor and commitment.

Open-Mindedness and Humility

Teacher leaders are careful not to become stuck in their own ideas. They actively solicit the thoughts of others and ensure that those ideas receive careful consideration. In doing this, of course, they demonstrate the skill of looking at evidence, and indeed, they help specify what would even count as evidence of the success of a proposed approach. But as a disposition, open-mindedness conveys a willingness to consider alternatives rather than approaching colleagues with a full-fledged program that they are trying to convince colleagues to adopt. Such an approach may feel to other teachers like a solution in search of a problem.

In addition, open-mindedness is accompanied by humility. Teacher leaders don't assume that their own idea is the best one or indeed that a proposed course of action will turn out to be the best approach. They are quite willing to admit that they don't know everything and that information may surface that would cause a shift in their plan. This open-mindedness and humility, of course, are consequences of a deep respect for colleagues and a commitment to collegiality. Respect and collegiality help to prevent the phenomenon, noted by some educators, of an energetic and skilled teacher who has lots of good ideas but a personality that can only be described as obnoxious. Teacher leaders who genuinely respect their colleagues and who convey the notion that the best ideas emerge from collective effort are rarely offensive to others.

Courage and Willingness to Take Risks

At times, teacher leaders must go out on a limb; success is not always guaranteed. In taking a new approach or persuading others to join in a project, they may have to go against the grain of traditional practice. Furthermore, they may be called on to gently and tactfully confront negativity or resistance from colleagues. Indeed, sometimes teacher leaders must find ways to challenge the larger school culture if it is characterized by cynicism and professional jealousy. The teacher leader is willing to swim upstream in such situations when the goal warrants it. Such actions require courage; school improvement is not for the faint of heart.

The connection between the courage of teacher leaders and the broader school culture is close. In order for educators to take risks, they must operate in an environment in which such courage is valued, where they are safe. This environment is established, by and large, by the administrative staff. But even within such a safe environment, not every teacher has the stomach to try a new approach, particularly one involving a significant departure from current practice; teacher leaders do.

Confidence and Decisiveness

Teacher leaders are individuals who have experienced success in their lives, frequently through their own hard work. Thus, they are reasonably confident of success in the future, provided they don't make avoidable mistakes. This expectation of success gives them a degree of confidence that rubs off on others; it is contagious. Everyone wants to be associated with a successful project; by conveying confidence, teacher leaders persuade others to join in the effort.

Confidence contributes to both courage and risk taking. Educators are not likely to step out and try something new if they do not have confidence in their ability to pull it off. So an underlying confidence is essential for teacher leaders: Confidence in their skill as teachers, confidence in their skill in thinking through a new approach, and confidence in their skill in persuading colleagues to join them.

Accompanying confidence is decisiveness. Teacher leaders know that when all is said and done, when the extensive discussions have run their course, action is necessary. This requires decisiveness in the face of uncertainty. Such decisiveness is accompanied, of course, by openness to the changing situation and conditions. It is not rational to pursue a course when it has become clear that it is not successful. So decisiveness is always accompanied by flexibility. But teacher leaders do not allow uncertainty to paralyze them and keep them from taking a course of action they believe to be the right one.

Tolerance for Ambiguity

Projects undertaken by teacher leaders are rarely planned in detail in advance. Instead, they are undertaken in response to a need or an opportunity and are subject to multiple midcourse corrections. It is in the nature of school improvement that many of the important issues can neither be known in advance nor planned for in detail. Therefore teacher leaders, in convincing colleagues to participate in a project, are inviting people to join them on a journey. They must be comfortable with the unstructured nature of the endeavor and be able to make adjustments as needed. But more important, teacher leaders do not feel the need for a detailed roadmap before the journey begins. They are able to go with the flow and are able to coordinate seemingly disparate aspects of a situation in their minds simultaneously. Teacher leaders can't be rigid in their approach.

Creativity and Flexibility

Teaching and learning are complex endeavors, and schools are complex places. Even if an educator encounters a program or practice that seems to have merit and wants to implement it in her own setting, it is unlikely to be able to be imported wholesale. At the very least, the program or practice will have to be modified to fit the environment. Some situations won't have models; in those cases, educators must create their own solutions. Teacher leaders are able to think creatively and flexibly and can encourage their colleagues to do the same.

Few projects move along as planned; adjustments are needed. Teacher leaders don't become trapped by their idea, sticking with it even in the face of evidence that it should be modified. They are flexible, able to stay true to the goal but willing to adjust the approach as needed.

Perseverance

Although flexibility is important, so is perseverance. A lot of success in implementing a new approach consists of holding firm even in the face of initial difficulty or resistance. The first attempt at anything is, practically by definition, more difficult than subsequent efforts will be. Everything is unknown and unfamiliar, and there are no established patterns. But as time goes on, routines are established and educators become more comfortable in the new practice.

Perseverance is not the same as stubbornness, of course; it must be tempered by flexibility and informed by reflection. But assuming that such reflection and flexibility are present, then an attitude of not giving up can inspire confidence in others. It gives them the strength to stay the course when they may be tempted to abandon it.

Willingness to Work Hard

Teacher leaders know that projects don't take care of themselves. They must be planned and implemented. Good ideas, without the hard work of planning and implementation, remain just good ideas. Real change, as Adam Urbanski (2004) has famously reminded us, is real hard. But teacher leaders are not only willing to work hard; they devise ways to work smart. And as noted above, they persevere in the face of setbacks and obstacles.

◇◇◇◇◇◇◇◇◇◇◇◇◇◇◇◇

These dispositions are not displayed one at a time by teacher leaders; rather, they constitute a cluster of traits and ways of looking at the world that tend to reinforce one another. Teacher leaders are confident, open-minded, enthusiastic, optimistic, and flexible. They persevere and are willing to work both hard and smart. These traits, as much as the specific ideas teacher leaders bring to a project, motivate their colleagues to join in and stay with that project.

All three teachers described in Chapter 1 displayed these traits. They approached their projects with energy and enthusiasm, optimistic that their efforts would yield positive benefits. They were open-minded to new approaches and persevered in their pursuit of a goal. And in convincing others to join them in the effort, they were not only persuasive but they also demonstrated both creativity and flexibility. Tom, in particular, was also courageous; he offered his own teaching as the first example of practice for his colleagues to examine. Taking that sort of risk required courage and trust in his colleagues that they would not abuse his vulnerability. All these dispositions, in addition to the skills described earlier, embody what it takes to be a successful teacher leader.

The dispositions of teacher leaders as described here also contribute to exemplary teaching. In their work with students, excellent teachers are also optimistic, confident, flexible, and creative. The dispositions are the same; teacher leaders simply exhibit them in the context of leadership activities with their colleagues.

The Administrative Role

Teacher leaders do not work alone; their activities and projects are facilitated by strong and sensitive administrative engagement. Some of the essential roles played by administrators concern creating an environment and culture in which teacher leadership can develop; that is the focus of Chapter 4. In addition to promoting a positive and professional culture, how do administrators contribute to the work of teacher leaders?

Some teacher leaders report that the best administrators, from their point of view, are those who take a *laissez-faire* attitude toward teacher activities; these teachers report, favorably, that the principal stays out of their way. In some situations this attitude may help teacher leaders accomplish what they want to do. But a weak administrator could actually thwart the work of energetic teacher leaders. And an inflexible administrator following a highly bureaucratic, authoritarian style might discourage initiative on the part of teachers. While a weak administrative style might, in general, be better for teacher leaders than a dictatorial one, it is hardly optimal. Better than either is an administrator who actively supports and promotes the development of teacher leadership, who honors the contribution of teachers to instructional improvement, and who supports teacher leaders in their work.

In supporting teacher leaders, the role of administrators can be, and ideally is, important; what that role is, and how administrators can do it, is described below.

Set the Tone and Culture and Maintain the Vision

Although every member of the professional staff has a responsibility to respect the school's vision for student learning and to promote a culture of hard work, respect, and professional inquiry, administrators play a unique role. They are, after all, the official leaders of the school; their approach to issues of culture matter, and they matter a lot. Site administrators convey messages from district headquarters; they let teachers know what districtwide projects and mandates must be implemented. It is the administrator's responsibility to ensure that the entire staff understands and demonstrates commitment to the school's goals for student learning. While teacher leaders exercise their influence by persuasion, administrators have the authority of their position, when needed, to back up requests. The matter of culture, and the administrator's role in establishing it, is the subject of Chapter 4.

Convey and Build Confidence in Teachers

Teachers unaccustomed to taking initiative and exercising leadership may not believe that their ideas will be valued. They may not even be sure their ideas have merit. Administrators are in a position to send important signals to teachers that their ideas are important and that the teachers play a critical role in improving the school's program. These signals are sent in many ways; among the most effective are the informal ones, in which principals invite individual teachers to discuss more fully an idea the teacher has put forward. Alternatively, principals can give public recognition—for example, at a faculty meeting—to an idea that has come from a teacher and invite others to explore it.

Clarify Ideas and Plan an Approach

A teacher may approach the administrator with the germ of an idea, a perceived opportunity to improve the school's program. But the idea is likely to not be fully developed. It may conflict or be redundant with another initiative of which the teacher is unaware. The principal has an important responsibility to help the teacher leader hone the concept and develop a plan of action that is likely to succeed. This can take the form of asking clarifying questions, suggesting ideas, proposing alternatives, or helping to talk it through. Whatever form it takes, the engagement of the principal conveys professional respect and the sense that the teacher's thoughts and ideas are valued. Moreover, the resulting approach is likely to be superior to the original, simply by having the benefit of another's perspective and expertise.

Marshal Support from Downtown

Some initiatives can be implemented solely within a school; others need to be condoned by others in the district organization. Principals play an important role as advocates for projects initiated by educators in their school, ensuring that the projects are understood and supported by the larger administrative team. There may be opportunities to coordinate an effort with an initiative in another school; discussions across the entire district can bring these opportunities to light.

Locate Additional Resources

Administrators are typically connected with district and other external resources that can support an initiative. Such advocacy is essential. In addition, administrators frequently have access to other support networks, such as business roundtables or foundations. Teacher leaders themselves, of course, might make a presentation to a business or parent group. However, the resources are not likely to be liberated on the strength of a teacher's presentation alone; the principal's sponsorship is essential.

Demonstrate Support to the Ranks

Teacher leaders, when they embark on a project or an investigation, are taking a professional risk. They are demonstrating initiative and assertiveness in front of their colleagues, and they may be regarded with suspicion by the old guard. This is partly a cultural issue. But at the least the administrator, by publicly offering support to the teacher leader, can send a signal to the entire faculty that good ideas and good questions are valued. It is a concrete way in which the administrator can support the efforts of a teacher leader.

Present Innovations to the Public

Any new practice must be understood and valued by the public, particularly by the parents of students involved. Insofar as the principal is the official voice of the school, it is important that the message emanate from the principal's office. Teacher leaders may be involved in this effort, but it cannot happen without the principal.

As mentioned briefly in the leadership stories in Chapter 1, Margaret's, Elena's, and Tom's principals facilitated the projects they undertook. The administrators helped Margaret and Elena hone their ideas after they had given them preliminary shape. Tom's principal provided time at a faculty meeting for his initial presentation. When necessary, the administrators provided or located resources to pursue the ideas; they gave the school's official stamp of approval to the ideas as they were being developed. The administrators did much more than get out of the way; they played positive and supportive roles in the evolution of these teacher leaders.

Teacher leaders, in exercising their leadership, follow some general behavioral patterns. Regardless of the setting in which they work or the area of school life in which they operate, teacher leaders display the skills and dispositions described here. Some may be more important in some settings than in others, but they all come into play to some extent.

In sum, true teacher leadership is exercised spontaneously and may be demonstrated by any teacher in the school; it is not conferred by role. Furthermore, it is not a permanent state; depending on their personal and professional situations, teachers may elect to be involved in a leadership effort one year but not another. Lastly, teacher leadership is fluid. Once a teacher has demonstrated certain skills, he establishes credibility with colleagues and is recognized as a person who get things done. And in getting things done, in improving the school's program, teacher leaders demonstrate certain skills and dispositions.

4

School Culture

A framework for teacher leadership is not complete without attention to the culture of the school in which such leadership is exercised. This culture determines, to a large degree, the extent to which teachers will be able to acquire and exercise skills of leadership. In addition, when teacher leaders exercise their influence in the school, they do so in specific areas of school life. For example, they might work with their colleagues to start a new practice or they might take initiative in establishing a business partnership.

While the implementation of a new practice represents the exercise of leadership, a *good* initiative reflects important aspects of the school's culture, such as a guiding vision of high-level learning for students. Therefore, all leadership activities take place within a cultural context encompassing the school's culture and ethos. This culture influences not so much *what* people do but *how* they do it. The school's culture affects how individuals treat one another, the expectations people have for their own and others' behavior, and the belief structure underlying school practices. For a more thorough investigation of school culture, see Deal and Peterson (1999).

The culture of the school has an important influence on how the school operates and the extent to which it can achieve positive results for its students. This is neither a trivial matter nor an afterthought. Rather, issues of school culture are pervasive; a dysfunctional culture can undermine the efforts of even the best-intentioned educator.

Given the pervasive influence of organizational culture and the importance of leaders in shaping culture, attention to culture is essential. The contributions of both administrators and teacher leaders are critical.

As anthropologists and experts in organizational development will attest, institutional cultures develop slowly and are remarkably resistant to efforts to change them. They are shaped by the behavior of everyone in the organization: students, staff, administrators, and parents. Schools have a certain feel to them, an electricity almost, that is evident to anyone walking in the door. A school can feel happy, productive, and welcoming, or it can feel negative and angry, with a poisoned atmosphere. Teachers feel either positive and optimistic about their work or frustrated that their expertise and efforts are not being used to best advantage.

Different aspects of the school's culture shape the tone of the organization. A positive culture inspires optimism and hope; a negative culture promotes cynicism and defeatism. This pervasive atmosphere is felt and reflected in the interactions between and among students, teachers, administrators, noninstructional staff, and parents. It is also shaped by the attitudes of staff toward external mandates and pressures; educators may feel themselves on the receiving end of endless requirements from the school district or from state and federal agencies.

Respectful Interactions

The most pervasive aspect of school culture concerns the manner in which individuals relate to one another. More than any other single factor, the manner in which people are treated influences their attitude toward an institution. Every person, as an individual and as a representative of a role, participates in the network of relationships within the school and school community.

Students

Schools are institutions created for the express purpose of educating the young people of a community. But in some schools, students are treated as inconvenient interruptions in what would otherwise be a pleasant environment. Teachers establish inflexible grading policies; administrators keep students waiting, even when they have summoned them to the office; attendance and discipline policies are punitive and seem to be grounded in negative assumptions about students and what motivates them; and students are treated with disrespect by their peers.

It is important to remember that students are no less human than the teachers; beginning in early middle school, many are actually larger than the adults. As human beings, students are entitled to respect as individuals; they deserve to be treated in a manner in which they can thrive. School practices must always be examined in regard to the extent to which they are respectful or demeaning, whether they promote student engagement or alienation, and whether they teach students the skills and habits that will serve them well as adults. Although the teachers and principal are the most significant adults who interact with students, they are not the only ones. Students encounter office staff, custodians, and other adults who work in the lunchroom and on the playground. It is important for the health of the environment that any adult who interacts with students does so in a respectful manner.

Another manifestation of respect demonstrated toward students concerns their treatment of one another. As every parent knows, students are not born being polite toward one another; demonstrating caring and respect is a learned skill. Students display their lack of respect for one another from being insensitive about another student's cultural heritage, to snickering when a peer offers an inadequate response in class, to teasing a student about unfashionable clothes, to serious bullying. In a school with a healthy school environment, students treat one another with respect.

An environment of respect for students is reflected in myriad small details about how things happen in a school: Adults don't talk down to students or cut them off when they are speaking; adults believe students' accounts of incidents and offer face-saving opportunities in case of conflict; adults trust students when students ask for access to a resource, for example, the office copy machine for an item needed for class.

A culture of respect toward students does not happen by itself; it must be cultivated. Students need to be *taught* to see events from another person's point of view and to make positive assumptions regarding one another's motives. Similarly, some of the adults in the school may have been treated as subhuman by adults in their childhood years. The concept, and the behaviors, of treating children as full-fledged human beings may represent a departure from their experience.

School leaders, whether teachers or administrators, model respect for students in everything they do and strive to incorporate the idea of respect into all aspects of the school. The schoolwide policies and programs put into place—for example, the approaches to discipline and attendance—must be grounded in assumptions of respect for students. Similarly, instruction and assessment practices are developed to honor the various cultural backgrounds and approaches to learning of different individuals. Students are included in the decision-making structures of the school so their perspectives are incorporated into the school's operations.

Colleagues

Teachers in a well-functioning school treat their colleagues with respect, both personal and professional. They neither engage in petty backbiting nor seek to score cheap points in public settings. Respect among colleagues reaches beyond the absence of negative behavior; colleagues are authentically respectful, particularly of differences.

◇◇◇◇◇◇◇◇◇◇◇◇◇◇◇◇

Professional educators recognize that educating students to a high level is not an easy matter; the particular challenges facing schools in the 21st century do not yield to simplistic solutions. Both teaching and the organization of schools are enormously complex; if it were easy to obtain good results, we would have accomplished our goal long ago. Furthermore, professional knowledge about practice continually evolves; educators know more today than they did a generation ago about effective teaching and curriculum organization. Hence, simply staying current with new developments is a significant undertaking.

The daily life of schools consists of multiple structures and patterns that are the legacy of decisions previously made. Some of these are oldies but goodies—practices that continue to be effective even in the face of new situations and evolving knowledge. Others are harder to justify on their merits and would benefit from focused examination and revision. Every staff, however, includes some teachers who, because of conviction or the absence of critical reflection, are not inclined to examine practices that are candidates for change. Hence, most school faculties comprise a mixture of the old guard and others who are typically, but not always, more recently minted and are eager to change everything. These groups occasionally clash over many matters, for example, those related to student discipline, schedules, or which students should be admitted to advanced courses.

Furthermore, there are in the internal deliberations of many disciplines long-standing debates about what best practice means. All educators are familiar with the reading wars; there are similar disagreements in many other parts of the curriculum.

What should be the relationship between inquiry and fact-based learning in science, for example, or conceptual versus procedural knowledge in mathematics? Educators frequently hold strong views on these matters and can usually come up with research findings to support their positions.

The net result of all this is that, for a variety of reasons, there is not an absolute consensus in many schools as to the best way to move forward. Teachers may have honest—and professional—disagreements about many issues confronting them, such as the way the curriculum and the schedule are organized, the most effective grading policy, and the most effective approaches to instruction. In working their way through these issues, members of the staff must be committed to an honest examination of evidence, a free airing of differences of opinion, and the presumption of positive intentions from everyone. Teachers must understand that their disagreements, which may be deep, are a result of professional differences in approach and that, although they may rest on different assumptions, they are all held with the best interests of students in mind. That is, teachers must treat one another with genuine respect and recognize that when they disagree with their colleagues, they may be challenging another individual's *ideas*, but they are not attacking the *person*.

Parents

In some schools, a culture has been established in which parents are, on the whole, seen as troublemakers who interfere with the real work of the school. Some educators forget that parents, having raised their children from infancy, know them well and can contribute to the school's efforts on behalf of student learning. Parents are, in the best sense of the term, partners with school personnel in ensuring student learning.

Parents of students are individuals in their own right and are deserving of respect. Students are, of course, the school's first clients. But parents are secondary clients; it is essential for the total life of the school that they feel honored and respected in their interactions with teachers, administrators, and the office staff. When parents are kept waiting in the office or are treated as part of the problem rather than integral to the solution, the school's efforts are less effective than they would be otherwise. When parents feel truly honored, when their perspectives are incorporated in the school's approach to their children, and when those who can devote the time and energy are invited to serve on the school's site council, they become essential advocates for the school among their friends and neighbors.

Noninstructional Staff

As with other groups in the school, the noninstructional staff play a critical role in creating and maintaining the ethos of the school. Indeed, in some schools, teachers report that it is the secretary and the custodian who really run the school. In addition, for many students, the interactions they have with the office staff, the kitchen staff, the custodians, and the playground aides shape their view of the school and of their place within it. When members of the support staff take an interest in students and convey that respect through their daily interactions, the students themselves grow from it. When adults take students seriously and trust them, students' sense of self is enhanced.

In addition to their interactions with students, noninstructional staff are important members of the school team. They are not, and should not be treated as, second-class citizens in ensuring that the school functions well. If the school is exploring a new attendance policy, for example, the office staff will have important contributions to make in ensuring that the new approach is feasible. The custodian may well have ideas on how to help students be more responsible in their treatment of the facility. Members of the noninstructional staff are part of the team and should receive the respect they deserve. The school's program and the general tone of the school will be the better for it.

◇◇◇◇◇◇◇◇◇◇◇◇◇◇◇◇◇◇

Teacher leaders don't create an environment of respect in a school on their own. Their role is critical, however, as are the roles played by students, instructional and noninstructional staff, and administrators. Teacher leaders are alert to situations in which individuals are being demeaned and know when their contributions are not being fully honored. They are able, in a tactful manner, to point out inconsistencies between a school's professed commitment to an environment of respect and the reality. Teacher leaders who point out such inconsistencies do so gently and professionally out of high regard for their professional colleagues, but in a manner that serves to remind others of the essential humanity of their students, the positive intentions of parents, and the contributions of the noninstructional staff.

All three teachers from Chapter 1 worked in schools with high levels of respect, and they displayed respect for the various groups with whom they came into contact. This respect was demonstrated most vividly in their interactions with colleagues: Margaret, Tom, and Elena all enlisted others in their thinking and planning and took time to listen carefully to others' views and to revise their ideas based on their contributions. In particular, Tom, in addressing a sensitive issue of classroom practice, demonstrated great respect for the vulnerabilities of his peers. In addition, Margaret and Elena, in presenting their respective plans for study trips and looping to parents, devoted sufficient time and attention to those presentations to ensure that their ideas were understood and that parent concerns could be addressed.

The School's Vision for Student Learning

A school's staff cannot hope to achieve high-level learning for all students if it neither aims to do so nor believes it to be possible. Therefore, a vision for student learning that drives school improvement efforts is an optimistic one, one that recognizes the intellectual potential of all students and regards the school's responsibility as that of setting the conditions for that potential to be realized.

This is not a naïve vision: Cognitive scientists concur that essentially all children are effective and efficient learners. By the time children enter school, they have amassed a vocabulary of about 3,000 words. It is true that some children, due to their language-rich environments, have a larger vocabulary than others. However, all children, whatever their backgrounds, are *learners,* and eager ones at that. There are virtually no intellectually lazy 5-year-olds, and yet there are lots of intellectually lazy 14-year-olds. Children have many experiences between the ages of 5 and 14, one of which is going to school. If educators were to merely retain the intellectual energy of children when they enter school, many of the motivation problems they report would disappear.

It must be recognized that not all school structures support student learning. Indeed, the manner in which students are assigned to classes and to groups within classes, the master schedule, the grading system, and even instructional practices may undermine the school's vision. Therefore, an unrelenting insistence on high levels of student learning and a commitment to translate that insistence to good school practices on a daily and hourly basis is an essential element of a successful school.

It is tempting, of course, to assign blame for lack of student learning on factors outside the school (Darling-Hammond, 1996). Indeed, approximately one-half the variance in student achievement can be attributed to external causes. But that does not imply that school success, defined as meeting high standards of achievement, is beyond the reach of large numbers of students. When students encounter difficulties in mastering complex material, as all students do from time to time, it is a challenge for the entire school to tackle. It is not a problem for a single teacher, or a single team or department; it is a challenge for everyone. Hence, we value collaboration and professional learning communities; some of the issues encountered are too complex for individual teachers to address on their own.

A vision of student learning and success drives practices throughout the school. And when revised practices yield positive results—when the most "unlikely" students do well—educators find that their long-held and sometimes unacknowledged beliefs about the potential of some students must be revised. In these situations, the mantra of "all children can learn" shifts from a hollow statement of belief to a reflection of reality.

A vision of student learning was the engine that drove the projects undertaken by Margaret, Tom, and Elena. Margaret knew that her students could derive a richer experience from the town's museum and could not rest until she had created a better mousetrap. If she had been content with her students' low-level learning and with having them traipse around the museum without learning much, she could have retained the previous approach. But she knew that a better result must be possible and that with the resources represented by the museum staff, her students could achieve a much higher level of understanding. So she acted on that belief and created an approach that everyone acknowledged to be far better than what it had replaced.

Tom, in helping his colleagues to examine their own practice, was motivated by what he considered unacceptably low rates of participation by girls and students of color. He held a vision of student learning that was not compromised by what he regarded as irrelevant considerations, and he worked courageously and diligently both to understand the situation and to remedy it. Elena, too, was motivated by a vision of school in which all students had the advantage of a caring teacher, one who was well acquainted with each individual and who could make adjustments as the conditions required. She recognized that there was an approach better than what the school had been doing previously, and she worked diligently to promote first conversation, and then action.

Student Culture of Hard Work, Responsibility, and Success

Every successful adult has learned the importance of hard work. Anything difficult to achieve, whether it is building a business or mastering trigonometry, requires a significant investment of physical and intellectual elbow grease. Furthermore, it is everyone's obligation to put in that hard work, rather than to assume that others will do it.

When schools take seriously their obligation to educate every student to a high level, when the school accepts no excuses for failure, the school is not discounting the value of hard work by students. Indeed, part of the challenge for schools is to establish systems in the school that encourage and even reward hard work. When combined with the previous element of culture (a prevailing vision of high-level learning), punitive policies toward grading, for example, are hard to justify. When students have the opportunity to earn a higher grade by learning complex material more thoroughly and retaking a test, they are more likely to do so than if their initial poor grade must stand regardless of any additional effort on their part. (This is not to suggest a policy of endless retakes; that is likely to promote procrastination. But reasonable opportunities to re-engage with material for the purpose of extending learning should not be discouraged.)

It should be noted that incentives are not the same thing as bribery. Using incentives to motivate students merely reflects structures that are designed to reward, rather than discourage, student application to learning. These structures might be in the homework policy, the school's policies toward tracking and grouping, and instructional practices that incorporate public displays of student learning. In all these areas of school life, students are either rewarded or not for the amount of energy they invest in their work.

Besides the responsibility for creating a culture of hard work, school personnel must also be responsible for establishing a culture of success. While recognizing that in order to succeed it is important to work hard, students also need to know that if they work hard, they can succeed. Students should never have the sense that "no matter how hard I work, I still get a *D*." Such a belief on students' part makes it only rational to give up and spend time with their friends rather than studying.

Recent research has illuminated the close connection between student views of intelligence and their willingness to work hard (Dweck, 1999). When students view intelligence as a natural endowment, something one is born with, they are less likely to apply themselves to complex learning than they are if they believe their success in learning to be a result of hard work. If students honestly believe that they are just not good at a certain subject—typically mathematics or science—then no amount of hard work will overcome that deficiency. Indeed, students who see themselves as possessing a natural ability in an area may be less likely to work hard (and to be seen to be working hard), because if one has to work hard, that must suggest that one is not smart in that subject. Interestingly, students in countries that score in the top rung in international assessments attribute their success in learning to hard work; U.S. students are more likely to attribute it to natural endowment or luck. The inclination to work hard is therefore a critical disposition to instill in our students. As D. Bruce Jackson (2003) has so well articulated it: "What matters most is that students come to believe deeply in their own capacity to master difficult academic material through sustained, thoughtful effort" (p. 582).

A culture of hard work, of course, must pertain to everyone, not just students. Administrators set the tone by working hard themselves and holding teachers to high standards. But teacher leaders play an important role also, first by modeling hard work on their own part and that of their students and then by encouraging their colleagues to follow suit. All teachers can convey high expectations for their students by handing back a paper that is sloppy or ill-thought-out, and saying that they know the student can do much better. Similarly, teachers, in their interactions with colleagues, must expect work of the highest standard and make efforts to constantly improve it.

Margaret and Tom, in particular, emphasized the concept of hard work in their projects related to study trips and eliminating the achievement gap. For example, when Margaret's students spent an entire week at the museum, they took a far more active role in what they learned there, formulating questions to ask the docents and developing theories about what the displays showed about life in earlier times. Their active engagement required application and energy on the part of students and contributed to the greater benefit they derived from the trips.

Tom and his colleagues, in changing their classroom practices, found that they had to address the issue of hard work directly. They needed to convince their students that learning difficult material is indeed hard work, but that by serious application they could master it. The teachers themselves, of course, had to believe that success was possible and that the students were up to the challenge. Student work is a critical piece of the puzzle of student learning, and the teachers recognized it as such.

Staff Culture of Professional Inquiry

Possibly the most important aspect of a school's culture from the point of view of encouraging teacher leadership is the culture of professional inquiry. Traditional professional norms, pervasive in many schools, reflect autonomy and privacy, leading to the feeling that to inquire about another teacher's practice is to suggest criticism. Such attitudes don't promote collegiality and professional learning.

It is well recognized, but little acted upon, that the greatest professional resource available to every school is the expertise of its teachers. Yet as valuable and extensive as this knowledge and experience are, they are rarely tapped for planning and improvement. Therefore, if educators are interested in improving outcomes for students, they must not ignore the expertise within their walls.

But there are other, more compelling reasons for schools to adopt a culture of professional inquiry. These reasons relate to teaching as a profession and to how teaching is regarded both within schools and in the larger community. No thinking person would entrust her health or finances to an individual who is not current in the fields of medicine or accounting. Ongoing learning is rightly regarded as one of the hallmarks of a profession. Teacher preparation and training, as in other fields, are merely the beginning of professional learning, which can be expected to continue throughout one's career. Unfortunately, the culture in many schools specifically undermines this expectation. Many teachers are careful not to rock the boat until they attain a continuing contract or tenure, and they then believe that their responsibility for professional learning is finished and that they can continue teaching with a minimal extension of skill for their entire careers.

The architecture and schedules of many schools reinforce the culture of independence and autonomy. Most teachers don't have frequent opportunities to interact with their colleagues; they have many demands on their time and extensive preparation for the next day's classes to complete. It therefore requires considerable discipline to make time for meaningful professional collaboration and inquiry. But it is much more than an issue of time; it is a question of values. Teachers must have the inclination to collaborate and learn from colleagues, and the culture must be sufficiently safe to permit the inevitable risk taking inherent in such conversations.

A component of a culture of professional inquiry is the norm of openness to change. Successful schools do not become frozen in old practices; the educators in them recognize the need for flexibility in achieving their goals. The new approaches to be used or tried are naturally informed by the results of professional inquiry—that is, they are grounded in professional obligations of examination of evidence. More important, there is a cultural openness to the examination of better ways of doing things, ways that might represent a significant departure from past practice.

The culture of inquiry is established first by the administration. In a school with a well-developed culture of inquiry, administrators ensure that every teacher is aware of an expectation for ongoing professional engagement. This is not a choice; it is integral to the work of teaching. But the parallel expectation must also be in place: When teachers take a risk and ask advice of a colleague or seek to improve their practice, the environment must be not only safe but encouraging.

The culture of professional inquiry must be established by administrators, but it is maintained and contributed to by teachers. They are the ones who must truly believe that their teaching is never perfect, that it can be improved. They must have or develop the disposition of critical examination of school practices that may be inhibiting student learning. They must adopt a sense of continuous improvement—the opposite of complacency. This attitude holds that no matter how successful a school is at the moment, it could always be better.

Teacher leaders have a particular responsibility for setting and maintaining the culture of professional inquiry. They are, after all, respected for their content knowledge and instructional skill; they have professional credibility. They hold themselves to high standards of professionalism. To paraphrase an old advertisement, when they speak, their colleagues listen. Teacher leaders approach their work in a spirit of inquiry, in anticipation that better approaches can be found.

All three teacher leaders described in Chapter 1 demonstrate a commitment to a culture of professional inquiry; they all regarded it as part of their responsibilities as a teacher to be continually seeking improvements in their schools and approaches to student learning. Margaret took on the traditional way of doing field trips, seeking a better approach and, eventually, enlisting the participation of teachers across the state. Tom, too, insisted that he and his colleagues must subject their practice to critical examination and institute improved practices to ensure improved results with their most vulnerable students. And Elena could have been content with the old schedule, but she recognized an opportunity to improve the school's program. She saw the constant quest for better approaches as an important aspect of her work as a teacher. All three of these teacher leaders operated on the assumption of professional inquiry, and in so doing made a significant contribution to that culture.

School culture, overall, sets the tone for teacher leadership. It influences not so much what teachers and administrators do, but how they think about what they do and the broader context within which they regard their work. The implications inherent in a school culture are profound: When teacher leaders work with their colleagues or make a presentation to a parent group, they do so with an underlying tone of respect. When teacher leaders propose a change to one of the school's policies or programs for students, the proposal is situated within a vision of high-level learning and hard work by students. School culture is not a small matter, and systematic attention to it from both teachers and administrators is a necessary condition for meaningful improvement. Given the nature of culture and the notoriously slow pace with which cultures change, this is not a short-term effort; it requires commitment over an extended period. It is this consideration, as much as any other, that reinforces the essential role of teacher leaders in promoting both school improvement and the professionalization of teaching.

A school's culture of professional inquiry establishes the ethos within which teacher leaders can emerge and initiate efforts regarding the school's program. But it is the other aspects of culture, including an environment of respect, a vision of learning, and a culture of hard work and opportunity, that help the projects undertaken by teacher leaders to actually *improve* that program. For example, a teacher initiative to implement a punitive grading policy, while representing a manifestation of teacher leadership, would not represent an improvement. Hence, we see the importance of school culture in ensuring the quality of the initiatives undertaken by teacher leaders.

How Teacher Leadership
Is Demonstrated

In understanding the work of teacher leaders, it is important to get specific. It is all very well, for example, to say that teacher leaders "work collaboratively." But what does that mean, specifically? What is it that they actually do? What are some examples?

Part II answers these questions. It offers concrete examples for each of the three areas of school life and each of the three settings in which teacher leaders exercise their skill. The areas of school life examined are schoolwide policies and programs, teaching and learning, and communications and community relations. Each area has several smaller components. Furthermore, examples are offered for each of the three settings in which teacher leaders operate: their own department or team, across the school, and beyond the school. These three settings are not intended to convey a hierarchy: Reaching beyond the school, for example, is not a more advanced level of teacher leadership than working with one's departmental or team colleagues. It is just different, and thus the sorts of activities in which a teacher leader is likely to be engaged are different.

The examples offered here are just that: examples. They are not intended to be a comprehensive listing of possible actions a teacher leader might take. Indeed, a comprehensive list would be impossible to compile. The examples are intended to prime the pump for further thinking by teachers and administrators. Teachers can use the information to determine how they could best exercise leadership in their own settings.

Administrators may benefit from understanding how they can influence and encourage the emergence of teacher leaders in their schools and districts.

The Appendix offers an audit that may help teachers and administrators in preparing for teacher leadership roles. An honest evaluation by educators and students can inform the journey.

5

Schoolwide Policies and Programs

As anyone who has been involved in school improvement efforts can attest, schools, even small schools, are immensely complex organizations. They include many interrelated components, all of which are themselves complex and composed of many individuals with independent views and values, but everything is organized around a common effort. It is in pursuit of the common effort that schools establish their policies and programs.

When a teacher joins the faculty of a school, these policies and programs (such as the grading system, the approach to professional development, and student activities) define their work to a large extent. That is, while teachers identify their principal responsibilities in terms of the students they teach and think of their professional work as that which happens within the walls of their classrooms, that work is affected by what occurs in the school beyond those walls.

The success of teachers' work with students is heavily influenced by the structures of the school and the opportunities available for them and their students. These structures and opportunities fall into several major categories: school organization and structure, student policies, student programs and activities, and staff programs. While these categories are traditionally classified as administrators' responsibilities, teacher leaders play a pivotal role in shaping each of these areas to maximize student learning.

In fact, the voice of teachers is essential to ensuring that these policies and programs are designed in an optimal manner.

Some aspects of a school's policies and programs remain principally within the administrator's responsibilities even in a school with active teacher leaders, including approaches to teacher evaluation, budgeting, staffing, and facilities use. However, even in these areas the views and perspectives of teachers, and especially teacher leaders, can make a substantial contribution to how those aspects of the school's program are designed. For example, if an important purpose of teacher evaluation is to encourage professional reflection and contribute to professional learning, it should not be regarded as something that the administrators do to teachers. Rather, it should be a collaborative effort in which teachers play an active role.

The categories of schoolwide policies and programs are described in the following sections.

School Organization and Structure

School organization and structure refer to all those fundamental aspects of how the school is organized for instruction: The organization of the school into subunits, the master schedule, and the assignment of different teachers to teach different courses or be responsible for different groups of students. These issues influence the tone of the building in the broadest possible way.

Organization of the School into Subunits

Very small schools typically exist as a single unit. With one or two classes at each grade level in an elementary school, for example, it is possible for every teacher to know virtually every student in the school. Student clubs can include students of different ages, and peer tutoring programs are simpler to arrange than in a larger school. In a large elementary school and in most middle and high schools, many educators have found it desirable to create smaller subunits, for example, instructional teams, houses, or schools-within-schools. These subunits typically correspond to specific areas or wings within the school; therefore, the physical structure of the building influences what can be accomplished organizationally.

Large elementary schools can be structured either as grade-level teams or as family teams, in which several teachers in adjacent grade levels (for example, two teachers of 2nd, 3rd, and 4th graders) form a team to work together with all their students.

Another practice at the elementary level concerns the move to a looping approach, in which a single teacher retains the same students over several years by moving with them, typically from 1st to 2nd, and then to 3rd grade, and then returns to the 1st grade for a new group of students. This is the approach that Elena, one of our teacher leaders in Chapter 1, proposed to her school.

At the middle school, it is not uncommon for the school to be divided into houses, frequently corresponding to a wing of the school in which students have instruction in all the core subjects; they go to other areas in the school for elective courses. Typically, each house contains one teacher in each of the core areas; they coordinate their efforts to a greater or lesser extent depending on the actual content of what they are teaching and their own strengths and preferences.

At the high school level, the typical subunits are the departments (for example, English, science, math). But some high schools, particularly very large ones, have instituted cross-disciplinary schools-within-schools, for example, a 9th grade school. Such an arrangement can help ease the transition of some students from the smaller environment of a middle school to the more impersonal culture that is typical of most large high schools.

Each arrangement has its advantages and disadvantages. Teacher leaders can play an important role in shaping the conversations with their colleagues, assembling relevant research, and helping to voice issues important to teachers that administrators might not consider or to which they might not give sufficient weight.

The Master Schedule

It is impossible to overstate the significance of the master schedule in shaping the educational experience of students and the professional life of teachers. The schedule defines the time available for teachers and students and therefore influences the type of engagement that students can have with what they are learning. At the elementary level, the schedule conveys powerful messages about the relative importance of different subjects, such as when reading is allocated 90 minutes per day and science receives a paltry 30 minutes twice (or once!) a week. Furthermore, the scheduling of special classes—art, music, and physical education, when these are taught by specialists in those fields—often has the effect of isolating those subjects and disrupting the flow of class activities.

At the middle school level, particularly if the school is divided into houses, the teachers themselves may determine their house schedule. However, the house schedule is affected by elective classes, which may interfere with sustained time for students to engage deeply with content. Many high schools have experimented with block scheduling, in which instructional periods are roughly 90 minutes in length, rather than the more typical 45 (or so) minutes.

All these different approaches have their advocates, and none is clearly superior to the others; again, it is a matter of balancing the consequences of each one and selecting the best option for a particular situation. As it is in the organization of the school's sub-units, the voice of teachers is essential to arriving at the best approach. In a supportive culture, teacher leaders may take the initiative in beginning the conversation.

Grouping of Students and Assignment of Teachers

Most schools have moved away from the rigid tracking of students that characterized schools in the 20th century. But while elementary reading groups are no longer labeled the "bluebirds" (largely predicting the population of high school AP English 10 years later), many schools find that some grouping of students into temporary skill groups—for at least portions of the day or for some subjects—helps ensure the success of all students. And most high schools offer courses as electives (either advanced levels of traditional academic subjects or specialty areas such as video production), affording students the opportunity to experience appropriate challenge or to pursue interests.

Any grouping of students other than random assignment involves decisions regarding which teachers work with which students. Of course, at the high school level, teacher expertise is a critical factor. But at other levels it is a less important factor, and assignments can be more flexible. Decisions about teacher assignment to groups of students, and indeed the manner in which students are grouped, are ones that can be left to teachers to work out, particularly when those discussions are guided by teacher leaders with a broad picture of the school's mission and vision.

At the high school level, where advanced courses are typically available for students who qualify for them and wish to make a commitment to doing the frequently substantial amount of work involved, decisions must be made as to the mechanisms of qualification. In many schools, these decisions are made by teachers, who invite certain students to enroll, or there is an expectation among certain groups of students that they will take certain courses. These practices frequently result in the patterns Tom (from

Chapter 1) observed in his school—much greater numbers and percentages of more affluent students in the advanced courses and girls underrepresented in mathematics and science.

School Decision Making and Governance

Few schools these days are run as administrative fiefdoms; virtually all school administrators establish structures (such as a leadership council or site council) both for making routine decisions regarding operations and for debating more substantive issues such as those described in this chapter. The leadership council is the group to which suggestions regarding a block schedule would be referred. Moreover, teachers increasingly play an important role even in those areas that are, in traditional schools, reserved for administrative fiat. These areas include staff hiring, budgeting, and teacher evaluation.

Schools with such representative governance typically establish a procedure by which teachers serve on decision-making bodies. Teachers may be elected by their colleagues, although in some cases the representation is more formal. For example, in many high schools, department chairs constitute the leadership council and individual members are selected by the administration. Similarly, at the elementary and middle schools levels, the teachers most active in school governance may be tapped by site administrators for these pseudo-administrative roles.

But where participation in site councils is voluntary and the decisions as to who is involved are left to teachers, teacher leaders play an important role in the area of schoolwide decision making and governance. They are willing to serve on site councils and contribute ideas for the better or smoother functioning of the school. They care deeply about the quality of the staff and volunteer to serve on a selection committee reading résumés, creating interview questions, and assessing candidates. They recognize the importance of schoolwide approaches to mentoring and professional development and make material contributions in those areas.

Some teachers are content to allow schoolwide decisions to be made around them and to accept the results without being part of the deliberation. But teacher leaders welcome the opportunity to engage with the issues and ensure that their schools' organizational structures maximize opportunities for student learning.

Schoolwide structures reflect important aspects of a school's culture. Interactions among members of the faculty (for example, in formal meetings to debate a possible change in the school schedule or in more informal interactions around the school) are respectful. The procedures established for student participation in advanced courses reward student commitment to hard work; teachers aim to encourage as many students as possible to stretch themselves in their work. The schedule is organized to include as few interruptions as possible so students can engage deeply with content.

◇◇◇◇◇◇◇◇◇◇◇◇◇◇◇◇

In other words, the school's organizational structures support the culture of high-level learning for all students and encourage students to fulfill their potential. All teachers, and especially teacher leaders, are alert to the impact of organizational structures on the school's ability to fulfill its mission. They don't accept such structures as fixed and divinely ordained; rather, they are a part of the framework of the school that can be adjusted to maximize student learning. Figure 5.1 provides examples of how teacher leaders work within the area of school organization and structure.

Student Policies

Just as the school's organizational structures define the broad use of space and time within the school, student policies define students' experience in the school as a whole. When adults recall their school days, many of their memories (particularly the negative ones) relate to a punitive grading or discipline policy, or to teachers whose homework assignments bore little relation to the course.

Most of the school's policies for students are established for the school as a whole. However, every teacher and every group of teachers who work together in a department or team interpret these policies for their own classes. They ensure that the policies and practices are implemented in a coherent manner and that they contribute to a positive school culture. Furthermore, for younger students, the policies and practices for students structure not only the students' relationship with the school as a whole but that of their parents.

The principal underlying concept regarding student policies is that they should serve to support student learning. They must respect students and the pressures on their lives. They must honor student needs and be designed so that student compliance with them is consistent with advancing student learning. Punitive policies simply encourage student efforts to circumvent them or subvert them to their own purposes. On the other hand, policies that support students in their development not only promote active compliance but also contribute to an overall culture of learning in the school.

FIGURE 5.1	
School Organization and Structure: Examples of Practice	

Emerging teacher leaders work with immediate colleagues to examine the school's organization and structure to maximize student achievement. For example, they might

- Encourage students to enroll in advanced courses.
- Participate in a team or school study group to propose a new organization of the school into subunits or a revision to the master schedule.

Setting	Established Teacher Leaders
Within Department or Team	Teacher leaders embrace opportunities to make the most of school organizational structures within their own departments or teams. For example, they might • Rearrange the team schedule so students have longer periods of time in each subject. • Determine when (if ever) it makes good educational sense to group students by ability or skill level. • Permit any students at the high school level who are willing to commit to the extra work the opportunity to enroll in an advanced course.
Across the School	Teacher leaders take the lead in examining school structures across the school. For example, they might • Invite colleagues to examine practices with respect to the organization of the school into smaller units and make a proposal to the full faculty. • Assemble research on the advantages (and disadvantages) of a block schedule, invite colleagues to share perspectives, and make a proposal to the full faculty and administration. • Initiate a project with colleagues from the department or from across the school to propose a new master schedule for the school. • Work with colleagues to establish a schoolwide policy on student access to advanced courses. • Serve as the team's representative on the school's site council. • Develop a staff survey on block scheduling.
Beyond the School	Teacher leaders participate in district, state, or national networks for critically examining school organizational structures. For example, they might • Serve on a district committee to formulate the district's policy regarding tracking and ability or skill grouping. • Work with representatives of other schools to propose a revised district specialist schedule for the elementary buildings.

One of the best ways to ensure active student compliance with policies and practices is to engage students in their development. Students are keenly aware of issues of fairness and are quick to point out when an approach is overly heavy-handed. Students understand the value of an orderly school environment and can easily appreciate the value of homework in providing additional opportunities for learning. As for grading, students know a reasonable grading policy when they see one, and their participation in the design or revision of the department's or school's approach to grading helps to ensure that it is both a good policy and one that students will accept.

Attendance Policies

The goal of a school's attendance policies is to ensure that students are in school as much as possible, on the assumption that they will not learn the curriculum when they are absent. Thus, some schools establish a policy that if students accumulate a certain number of absences during a school year, they cannot pass the course or courses for the year. A second goal of most attendance policies is also to encourage student punctuality; therefore, some schools have instituted policies under which a certain number of late arrivals is converted to a day's absence.

Of course, it is not advisable for students to attend school if they are sick and are carrying a contagious illness. Unfortunately, some students are not even aware they have an illness when it first sets in, and they spread it before they and their parents realize it. In addition to serious illness, which can keep students out of school for many days or even weeks, students are occasionally the victims of accidents (such as broken bones) that can result in extended absences.

In devising or revising the school's attendance policy, it is essential that the policy not be interpreted by students as punitive. It must also accommodate student responsibilities. For example, if a student has accumulated 16 absences early in the year, and 18 is the maximum allowable number, that student may take the view, What's the point? I may as well drop out! In addition, some students may have a situation at home that requires them to care for younger siblings who are ill when a parent must go to work. Students should not be penalized for shouldering such responsibilities.

Furthermore, students' responsibility for arriving at school on time can be an opportunity for learning. Those students who ride a bus have a particular challenge; they must be there exactly when the bus is due to come—they don't have the flexibility to leave (whether walking or being driven) a few minutes later. Therefore, bus riders can benefit from teacher-led discussions as to how to prepare the night before for the need to leave the house at a specific time in the morning—how to assemble school supplies and materials in a set location, determine the clothes to be worn, and other advice. These are life skills that carry into adulthood.

In general, attendance policies must simultaneously encourage student and parent responsibility regarding coming to school and flexibly accommodate individual student situations. This typically involves clear procedures to make decisions on a case-by-case basis in addition to general guidelines.

Discipline Policies

Every school needs an orderly environment in which students can work. Schools are crowded places; consensus as to what constitutes acceptable student conduct—in classrooms, in the corridors and lunchroom, on the playground, and on the buses—is important to ensuring access to learning for every student. Furthermore, some schools are plagued by bullying, making life miserable for the victims.

Discipline policies at the high school level also typically encompass such matters as what students may and may not store in their lockers, when and under what conditions they may leave the school grounds, and when they may access their lockers. Such policies are typically affected by the environment in which the school is located and whether students are likely to come in harm's way.

All schools attempt to instill habits of self-discipline in their students, but there is little consensus as to how this can be achieved. Some schools institute harsh zero-tolerance policies governing the infraction of school rules. Other schools have softer, more democratic approaches. While rigid rules are appropriate for certain matters, such as weapons possession, it is unlikely that, when applied to all areas, they encourage the type of self-monitoring behavior that is needed for the student to develop habits of self-discipline.

In addition, most educators recognize the relationship between student conduct and the quality of instruction. In general, when students are involved in meaningful learning, they are less likely to seek ways to circumvent the school's rules. Therefore, a school's approach to student conduct is both a contributor to and a consequence of the quality of instruction.

Homework Policies

Homework is one of the least understood components of a coherent educational plan. Well-crafted homework assignments can accomplish several important goals of a school: extending learning time and providing an opportunity for students to practice skills or rote learning (such as Spanish vocabulary). New conceptual learning is not appropriate for homework, since such learning must be mediated by a teacher. But once the foundation has been laid, homework assignments provide an opportunity for students to consolidate their understanding. Out-of-class projects offer many of the same benefits as homework assignments.

Caution should be exercised, however, when considering how to use homework in the best manner. For example, long homework assignments are not appropriate for young children; most primary teachers assign homework sparingly, if at all. Second, it is essential that students be able to complete the assignments independently. If an assignment requires adult assistance, it may be inequitable, as some students will have more reliable access to such assistance than others. It is not responsible to put students at a disadvantage if they don't have someone at home who can provide help. In addition, many teachers have experienced the phenomenon of parent-assisted science projects—it's not clear how much the students have really learned from them.

Homework assignments can help forge a link between home and school. Some disciplines lend themselves more to this than others—for example, students can interview their older relatives about what it was like to grow up during the 1960s or investigate the histories of their neighborhoods. Some mathematics assignments can use information from home, such as a survey by 2nd graders of which vegetables their families ate for dinner the previous night. When captured the next day, this simple information can be converted to graphs and charts, hypotheses can be formulated, and patterns can be observed.

Many parents appreciate guidance as to how they can best support their children in completing schoolwork. Such a topic is suitable for a parent evening, with written materials sent home to all families. It is an unfortunate fact that in some households, students find it very difficult to complete homework, even when they want to do so. There may be no quiet place in which to work, or they may be expected to care for younger siblings or prepare the evening meal. The school's responsibility in such situations is to offer as much assistance to families as possible, both by making a case for the importance of homework to learning and by offering practical suggestions for parents. In addition, some schools, as part of their programs of learning support, provide a protected time and space after school hours for students to work on their out-of-class assignments.

It is also important for educators to recognize the difference between completion and effort with regard to homework. Some students will make an honest attempt to do their homework but will run into a snag that prevents them from completing it. Teachers must have policies that acknowledge the effort and encourage students to be resourceful, such as by phoning classmates or seeking additional help from a homework hotline, but they should not penalize students who, in spite of a good attempt, have not been able to complete the assignment.

Lastly, flexibility is essential. Emergencies arise, and they arise in some families and communities more than in others. Students need to know that they may not abuse the understanding of their teachers; at the same time, when legitimate emergencies occur, students must not be penalized for factors beyond their control. Students need to know that homework or at least the honest effort to complete it is important for lots of reasons. Homework is important to ensure mastery of complex material, and it is important in developing self-discipline. However, when students fail to get their homework done, they need to know that their teachers, and the school as a whole, are reasonable.

Grading Policies

Much of a school's philosophy toward students is captured in its approach to grading; unfortunately, many schools' policies toward grading are not coherent (Marzano, 2000). Competing concepts are combined into a single letter or number with the result that no one is clear about what the grade signifies. Some teachers (primarily at the high school level) take pride in their "tough" grading policies, bragging, "No one ever gets an *A* in my class!"

But what does a grade even mean? Does a grade represent how well the student has mastered the material? Or how much effort the student has expended? Or how much improvement the student has demonstrated since the last grade was given? What is the role of extra credit? Can it be used to increase an otherwise low grade? And on what basis? Is it only that the student has done more work? If so, is this a legitimate practice? Lastly, are the principles behind student grades consistent across a school district, or a school, or even a single department?

A fairly strong case can be made for any one of the approaches to grading mentioned. The important challenge is to determine what a grade represents and to apply the principle consistently. And in order to do that, it is essential to be clear about the purpose of grades.

The first purpose, of course, is one of communication—to the students, to their parents, and to other institutions (especially colleges and universities). In that regard, it is essential that a grade represent student learning of the curriculum. Many parents are dismayed to discover as a result of state tests that their children are performing well below their peers even though they have been getting good grades. At the very least, grades must communicate about student learning.

Second, of course, grades can be and are used to motivate students to work hard. This can be important. Students may decide to forgo a night out with their friends to study for a test if they think it can make a difference. On the other hand, students need assurance that their efforts will pay off if they do work hard and learn the material, that there will be no tricks on the test. In other words, the effort must be worth it.

It is tempting to use grades to encourage students and to reward them for their hard work alone, even when it does not result in high-level learning. While it is important to acknowledge student effort, a better way to do that is through a separate grade or comment for effort, leaving the actual grade as simply a reflection of the quality and amount of student learning. The same reasoning applies to recognizing outstanding progress. Comments can be used to encourage students to continue in their efforts.

Grades are an important part of a school's culture, particularly at the secondary level. As such, the school's policies with respect to grading should be purposeful and designed to further the school's aims. Most schools could benefit from a hard look at how they grade students.

All student policies are important reflections of the school's underlying culture. If educators are sincerely trying to promote high-level learning for all students, they will seek to replace a punitive grading (attendance, homework, or discipline) policy with one that encourages student effort, one that is flexible and responsive to changing circumstances. They will ensure that the school's actions are consistent with its stated beliefs and that all the school's formal and informal policies support the development of student success and responsibility. This effort may require changes in policies that were developed at an earlier time, when values may have been different. Teacher leaders play a vital role in this area. They recognize the systemic nature of schools and the critical part that student policies play in shaping the culture of the school. They are not content to allow inherited policies to dictate the relationships between students and teachers in ways that might undermine the core mission of the school, and they work to change them where appropriate. Figure 5.2 outlines ways teacher leaders might work with their school's student policies.

Student Programs and Activities

Student programs bring the school to life for students. As much as teachers would like to believe that it is their brilliant instruction that motivates students to come to school each day, the truth is more likely something quite different. Most students, and former students, remember school in terms of the activities and programs in which they participated. Student efforts may also bring recognition to the school, as when a school's math team competes at the state level or the basketball team has a good season.

Student programs are different from the student policies described earlier in this chapter. Student policies set the context for formal learning, by specifying the attendance, grading, and discipline policies. Student programs, on the other hand, establish opportunities for students to expand their interests and skills, participate in out-of-class activities with classmates, and develop leadership skills. While some are linked to formal learning (e.g., a tutoring program for younger students), many are independent of the formal curriculum. Either way, the school is greatly enriched by them.

Curriculum-Based Activities

Some student activities are clearly curriculum based, such as a Spanish club or a literary magazine. Other examples are model U.N., a chess club, a math team, or a science team. A teacher leader recognizes an opportunity to engage students in activities that are not currently part of the school's offerings. An example of this could be a teacher's invitation to a poet-in-residence to spend a week at the school engaging all students in learning, reciting, and writing poetry. Such an effort could culminate in a parent evening, at which students read poems aloud to their peers and families. Such a plan, in addition to external resources, would require a significant amount of initiative as well as the coordination of the teacher leader's work with that of the other teachers in the school.

Other curriculum-based student activities are those in which students are enlisted to assist other students in their learning. Many elementary schools have implemented opportunities for older students to read to those in the kindergarten classes, or to assist the teacher in organizing hands-on science activities. Older students serve on a homework hotline, or actually tutor younger students. And as every teacher knows, when

FIGURE 5.2

Student Policies: Examples of Performance

Emerging teacher leaders work within their classes to examine and improve student policies. For example, they might

- Participate in team or departmental meetings to consider alternatives to the grading system.
- Try a new homework policy with their own students to determine whether it is more effective than the one they had been using previously.
- Encourage their own students to make use of the school's homework hotline.
- Establish clear guidelines for student conduct and maintain records that can contribute to the team's or department's deliberations about a broader discipline policy.

Setting	Established Teacher Leaders
Within Department or Team	Teacher leaders organize opportunities for examining student policies within their own departments or teams. For example, they might work with their colleagues to do the following: • Develop a departmental approach that motivates students to make a sincere effort to complete their homework. • Implement a new grading system that encourages students to take pride in their work. • Design a policy for student discipline that rewards students for assuming responsibility for their own and others' behavior.
Across the School	Teacher leaders organize efforts to examine student policies within the school. For example, they might • Coordinate the development of a new school policy regarding student attendance. • Work with representatives of other departments or teams to review the school's grading policy with the goal of revising it. • Coordinate an overhaul of the school's approach to homework. • Institute a buildingwide analysis of the school's discipline policy.
Beyond the School	Teacher leaders participate in district, state, or national networks for examining the impact of student policies on learning. For example, they might • Serve on a district committee to revise the district's approach to discipline. • Participate in a statewide conference or committee on the impact of student policies on learning and culture. • Contribute an article to a professional journal on the results of implementing a new grading policy. • Participate in a school district's formulation (or revision) of its promotion and retention policy.

you teach a concept, you learn it to a greater depth. Hence, engaging students in helping younger ones learn is likely to pay dividends in the older students' learning, as well.

Extracurricular or Cocurricular Activities

The best-known examples of cocurricular student activities are, of course, athletics. But there are others, including dramatic productions and class projects. A teacher might also see student interest in computer troubleshooting or a debate team. Such activities, while separate from the normal curriculum of the school, make a clear contribution to student learning in the regular school program.

Some schools have well-established programs of student clubs and activities, all of which require adult supervision and direction. In some schools, those roles are assumed by parent volunteers, but few schools can rely on such outside assistance. Rather, it is a matter for the staff to take up, determining which are the most important to enrich the students' total school experience.

In schools where teachers assume responsibility for the coordination of established activities and clubs, such as athletics or the school play, it is typically either part of their job (as with the drama teacher) or they are paid a stipend. Such stipends are intended to reflect the enormous amount of work involved in these extra pursuits, and the reputation that a school develops for excellence in such areas. A school's sponsorship of a chess team, participation in the model U.N., or the performance of its athletic teams serve to define the school in the eyes of others and offer important opportunities for its students.

Teachers who organize and manage established student activities often demonstrate leadership among their peers, even when they are paid a stipend for their work. But a more dramatic illustration of teacher leadership occurs when a teacher recognizes an opportunity to institute a new student program. For example, a teacher might introduce students to a new sport or establish a class project to raise money for an improvement to the school.

Student Leadership

Some of the activities students remember long after they leave school are those that afford them the opportunity to develop their own leadership skills. Even elementary schools are able to establish programs involving older students, in roles such as science lab assistants who organize and prepare materials for the teachers. Opportunities abound in middle and high schools, from student government, to a student chapter of

Habitat for Humanity, to a peer advisor program. Furthermore, students can actively participate in determining student policies. When such involvement is invited and encouraged—for example, requesting student participation in revising the school's approach to grading—students often surprise their teachers with the thoughtfulness of their contributions. Students at all levels benefit from participating in school governance, often as a participant on the student council or as a member of the school's site council. The benefit to students is greatest when the issues they address are truly significant.

In addition, students can be active investigators of school life. If a school faculty were interested in exploring issues of student culture (e.g., learning whether students felt they were treated fairly or with respect), students could make a material contribution in the design of a survey instrument. Naturally, their views would be solicited, but in addition, students themselves would have good suggestions as to how the questions should be framed to communicate with other students.

Student leadership can extend beyond the school. For example, in a school in Vermont, members of a student club collaborated with the school maintenance staff and a local waste management company to organize a schoolwide recycling program (McKibben, 2004).

Community Service

The recognition of the value of community service has led many high schools (and indeed some states) to institute a service requirement for students as necessary for graduation. This requirement recognizes the value of service for students: It enables them to see into the lives of others, frequently those who are less fortunate than they. It also is a testament to the value of service in clarifying what is important and in making a contribution to the community and people's lives. Furthermore, by participating in community service, students get a view of the agencies that offer the services and the people who work in them as doing a different, clearly important, kind of work.

There are a number of rationales for including service learning in the life of the school. Underneath them all, however, is the notion that schools are not just places where students go to learn; they are places from which students and teachers go forward into the community to make it a better place. In these service efforts, they make a contribution to the common good and students are not regarded as "problems to be managed, or resources only for the future" (Barone, 2003). They can make a contribution *now*. When students are involved in challenging situations in real-world settings, they acquire an appreciation for the issues people in their community deal with. This awareness can lead to a heightened sense of self and the development of an ethic of caring. Students develop a deeper respect for both human differences and similarities. Furthermore, by engaging in service learning opportunities, students are exposed to the responsibilities of citizenship in a democratic society.

It is not only high school students who can benefit from community service. Many elementary and middle schools also have outreach efforts involving volunteering in a soup kitchen or assembling Thanksgiving baskets. Students can be introduced early to the fun of collaborative work and the rewards of service.

U.S. society is filled with jobs for which students of various ages are suited. Some require skill, such as helping build a house with Habitat for Humanity, and therefore suggest a sustained commitment so the needed skills may be acquired and applied. Others require less specialized knowledge, such as visiting residents in a nursing home. Some, such as volunteering after school to tutor younger students, involve a commitment to another individual, and therefore should not be taken lightly. Activities such as nursing home visits, if they are conducted over time and with the same individuals, can also result in meaningful cross-generational relationships.

There is virtually no limit to service opportunities for students, but they need to be located and cultivated. Many adults in the community do not initially think of students as a source of volunteers, but once introduced to the idea, they embrace it willingly. However, the contacts must be made; that is typically a job for a teacher leader.

Teachers who organize student programs make a valuable contribution to the school. Once these are recognized as jobs, they may be eligible for a stipend. At the outset, however, these jobs are usually the brainchild of an inspired teacher who sees an opportunity—a teacher leader. In getting it going, in formulating an idea, in persuading colleagues to join the effort, and in marshaling resources, these teacher leaders display all the skills and dispositions described in Chapter 3. Figure 5.3 lists ways in which teacher leaders can affect student programs in their schools.

Staff Programs

Schools are not simply organizations where adults organize things for students. They are also places where adults organize things for themselves for the benefit of their students. A healthy school environment, it is now recognized, is one in which teachers are

FIGURE 5.3

Student Programs: Examples of Performance

Emerging teacher leaders work within their own classrooms to engage their students in rich student programs in the school. For example, they might

- Encourage students to participate in a tutoring program offered in the school.
- Elicit their students' opinions on new ideas for programs under consideration.

Setting	Established Teacher Leaders
Within Department or Team	Teacher leaders organize opportunities for student programs within their own departments or teams. For example, they might - Organize clubs within the team or department for students from all classes. - Establish student leadership roles across the team or department. - Create an intramural sports team to challenge students from other teams or departments in the school. - Enable students in science class to create an environmental education resource on unused land on the school campus. - Arrange for students from the team or department to contribute toys to a children's hospital. - Coordinate a program where science students create signs for storm drains with the message "Dump No Waste: Drains to River" for a local conservation foundation.
Across the School	Teacher leaders organize opportunities for student programs within the school. For example, they might - Establish a student government where none has previously existed. - Work with colleagues to establish clubs during a time of the day in which students are not productively engaged. - Coordinate opportunities for students to exercise their skills beyond the normal school program, for example, in a debate team or a chess team. - Initiate a student tutoring program. - Organize a big brother/big sister program in the school. - Introduce a new sport to the school. - Organize students to volunteer in the community library. - Solicit homemade craft items from school parents, organize a sale with students, and donate the money to a local animal shelter.

Setting	Established Teacher Leaders
	FIGURE 5.3 **Student Programs: Examples of Performance** *(continued)*
Beyond the School	Teacher leaders participate in district, state, or national networks for the larger establishment of student programs. For example, they might • Serve on a district or state committee to institutionalize the debate team. • Coordinate with educators from other schools or districts to implement student opportunities for leadership, such as a peer leadership program. • Work with representatives from other districts to organize a statewide program for students, such as a debate competition or a Russian club. • Represent the school in a district- or statewide program for drug-free schools. • Represent the district at a state conference exploring the effects of student programs on achievement.

productively engaged in meaningful work and have ongoing opportunities to enhance their knowledge and skill. Schools are also places where teachers are validated *as people,* where they feel affirmed as a member of a team. Here we'll describe several different categories of staff programs.

Recruitment and Hiring

Although traditionally reserved for administrators, the area of teacher recruitment and hiring is important to teachers. They recognize the importance of attracting exceptional teachers to the school. It is essential that new recruits have skills that will complement those of teachers on the staff and that they bring new strengths to the faculty. Teachers also want to be sure that new teachers will carry their weight in the hard collective work of the school.

Furthermore, when the opportunity arises to hire a new principal, teachers have an interest in ensuring that the strongest candidate is hired. In some districts, teachers have little influence over these decisions, but in places where they do, the resulting decisions are likely to be better than without their input.

There are many steps in recruiting and hiring, whether seeking teachers or principals: reading and screening résumés, creating and adapting interview questions, conducting interviews, contacting references, reviewing portfolios and videos, and deliberating about the candidates. Teacher leaders may participate in some or all these activities; time that most conclude is well spent.

Professional Development

Professional development is a broad term that applies to teacher participation in programs designed to expand teachers' knowledge and promote higher levels of student learning in the school. It can include such things as seminars and workshops, collaborative work with colleagues, mentoring, and supervision of student teachers. Most professional development concerns instruction and student learning. But there are other types as well, such as workshops on student drug use or patterns of child development. These topics have some impact on student learning, of course, but they are not directly linked to teachers' instructional skills.

The manner in which professional development is organized in a school reflects the school's culture of professional inquiry and the de-privatization of practice. Opportunities for professional learning are widely dispersed throughout the school and should not be interpreted to suggest that a teacher is not performing adequately. Rather, participating in professional learning should be regarded by all teachers as integral to the work of teaching.

There has been abundant research on the characteristics of effective professional development. It is well recognized that much of what has been offered in the past—one-shot workshops, university courses—has little impact on classroom practice. Instead, it is important for professional development offerings to serve the following purposes:

- Engage teachers in professional conversation
- Permit teachers to use new approaches in their classrooms
- Encourage teachers to learn from one another
- Include follow-up and coaching
- Be embedded in the work of the school
- Contribute to the intellectual capital of the school

Professional development thrives in a school when it is supported by initiatives at the district and state level. Exemplary professional development can happen in a school in the absence of those initiatives, but it is far more likely to occur when it is supported more broadly. This support refers to a culture for professional learning and to more practical matters, such as resources to pay for released time or external consultants.

Teacher leaders understand the essential role that professional development plays in the life of a school; they know that it energizes staff and contributes to the cumulative wisdom of a school's faculty. They are themselves active learners, always seeking to increase their understanding of how diverse students learn complex content. In addition, teacher leaders understand that a school's effectiveness with its students depends on the skill of every member of the faculty. Therefore, they work steadily but sensitively to engage all members of the staff in important professional learning.

Site administrators play a significant role in supporting school-based professional development and the work of teacher leaders in promoting that learning. Administrators are frequently the ones who know what is coming along from the district, and they are the ones ultimately in charge of the school's schedule and budget. Therefore, when teacher leaders want to exercise initiative in the area of professional development, the site administrator is a key individual to be convinced of the approach and to assist with the planning.

While teachers are the most critical members of the staff in influencing student learning, professional development extends to other members of the staff. For example, a teacher leader may determine that the aides' skills in supporting their work with students could be strengthened, and then work out a way to provide that training. Or it may become apparent that the school's secretary is conveying a punitive attitude toward parents; a teacher leader could, through coordination with the principal, work to change the secretary's demeanor.

Mentoring, Coaching, and Teacher Evaluation

Teacher development is supported by programs of mentoring and coaching. These may be organized by the district, but they are implemented in each school. Good mentoring and peer coaching programs are much more than buddy systems; those serving as mentors and coaches need substantive training to carry out their roles in a supportive and nonjudgmental manner. Furthermore, most educators who have participated in mentoring and peer coaching find that they—the mentors and the coaches—benefit in ways they did not expect. They frequently report that their own teaching has improved!

Even teacher evaluation, a domain traditionally reserved for administrators, can benefit from the voice of teachers in its design. If teachers are to benefit from a system of teacher evaluation, it must afford opportunities for teachers to reflect on their practice and engage in professional conversations with colleagues. While it is true that the actual evaluation of teacher performance is an administrative function, it is strongest when teachers are actively involved in self-assessment and analysis of their own teaching (Danielson & McGreal, 2000).

◇◇◇◇◇◇◇◇◇◇◇◇◇◇◇◇

When educators consider school improvement efforts, the programs for staff are sometimes taken for granted. But they require the same deliberate planning and implementation as any other component of the school's program; teacher leaders play a critical role in this vital area. The area that comes to mind is, of course, that of professional development; the role of teacher leaders is absolutely essential there. But teacher leaders play a part in the full range of staff programs, ensuring that the climate for faculty is as vibrant as it is for students. Figure 5.4 lists ways in which teacher leaders can work in the area of staff programs.

Social Programs

School life for faculty is not all work and no play; schools with a vibrant faculty culture include opportunities for teachers to participate in nonwork activities, such as an evening at the theater, a concert, or just a party. Camaraderie is stimulated when colleagues are able to depart the usual work environment and interact with each other in more social settings, such as during a miniature golf game or a cookout at the local pool.

Of course, social programs require organization. Someone has to make the roster for snacks for faculty meetings or for Friday morning recognitions. Faculty birthday celebrations require someone to organize them. Teacher leaders frequently step into these roles. They recognize the value of social activities to cement team relationships, and they help ensure a healthy climate in the school.

FIGURE 5.4
Staff Programs: Examples of Performance

Emerging teacher leaders work with immediate colleagues to participate in opportunities for professional learning. For example, they might

• Help plan a workshop for colleagues.

• Attend workshops and courses offered by outside groups to enhance their own skills.

• Join professional organizations for their own subject or level.

Setting	Established Teacher Leaders
Within Department or Team	Teacher leaders organize active staff programs within their own departments or teams. For example, they might • Review résumés or serve on an interview committee for the department or team. • Organize a professional development opportunity for their team or department. • Organize an orientation session for teachers new to the department or team. • Circulate an article relevant to the team's work. • Develop a team or departmental program for celebrating staff birthdays.
Across the School	Teacher leaders organize opportunities for professional development within the school. For example, they might • Participate in the hiring process for a new principal. • Organize a professional development course for the school. • Organize an orientation session for teachers new to the school. • Serve as the building liaison for student teachers. • Initiate a support group for candidates for National Board certification. • Coordinate the year's schedule for outside speakers at faculty meetings. • Plan TGIF activities for colleagues.
Beyond the School	Teacher leaders participate in district, state, or national networks for professional development. For example, they might • Serve on a districtwide professional development committee. • Design an instrument to determine district needs for professional development. • Represent the district on a statewide professional development body. • Play an active role in professional organizations at the state or national level. • Make presentations at state or national conferences of professional organizations. • Organize professional development courses to support district initiatives. • Represent the district at national conferences (e.g., subject or grade-level specific).

6

Teaching and Learning

Teaching and learning is, arguably, the centerpiece of any school; student learning is, after all, the *raison d'être* of education. A school is only as good as the instructional program it offers to its students and the results it obtains. While schoolwide policies and programs set the stage for the instructional program, the real magic of education happens every day in every classroom. To be sure, schools are also centers of their communities, and local residents frequently display a fierce loyalty to them. But in the end, a successful school is one that delivers a superior instructional program to its students, and the heart of that program is teaching and learning.

Teacher leaders are in a strong position to influence the school's instructional program. Teachers are the school's experts in the subjects they teach and in the patterns of learning of their students. No school can offer an exemplary instructional program to its students without the devoted work of its teachers. Teacher leaders, by mobilizing the energy of their colleagues, have a significant influence on the quality of that program.

A school's approach to teaching and learning involves several interrelated aspects: a focus on results, curriculum, assessment, and teaching. Teacher leaders make material contributions to improvement in all these areas. However, the efforts of teachers and teacher leaders are a bit different from their contributions in the other aspects of this framework, such as schoolwide policies and programs, and communication and community relations. In those other areas, a project or initiative is typically confined (at least primarily) to one area or another. That is, a teacher leader might initiate a discussion of the school's discipline or grading policy, or might propose a new student program to enrich the school's offerings. The same goes for communications and community relations: a teacher leader might devise a new business partnership or organize a schoolwide event for parents.

This segmentation is not possible in teaching and learning. Results, curriculum, assessment, and teaching are completely intertwined, and any individual effort will typically have elements from all four components. That is, when concentrating on results, a team or department, following the initiative of a teacher leader, might determine that the situation they have uncovered is the consequence of a gap in the curriculum or the result of inadequate formative assessment as students are exploring the topic, or that it could be improved by different instructional strategies. Similarly, if a school were to commit itself to greater integration of its curriculum (a curriculum matter), such an effort would have enormous implications for both assessment and instruction, as well as yielding (one hopes) improved results. Any specific effort, such as a study group to analyze student work and improve practice, may include several elements from the area of teaching and learning. Therefore, while the different aspects of teaching and learning in which teacher leaders might become involved (at the levels of their own team, the entire school, or beyond the school) are described separately for the purpose of analysis, it should be understood that they occur simultaneously.

With that understanding established, the four areas of teaching and learning are described individually in the next sections.

A Focus on Results

Any improvement of a school's instructional program must be based on information. For educators who are accustomed to making incremental or superficial changes in their offerings, a focus on information and data may represent a significant change. It is essential to know whether *each student* is making adequate progress, however, and the only way to know that is through the collection and analysis of information.

De-Privatization of Practice

Of course, an orientation toward results (that is, the "output" of education) rather than what educators *do* (the "input" of education) suggests that these results are publicly known. That is, a focus on evidence requires that educators de-privatize their practice and work together to improve outcomes. This creates apprehension among some teachers, who may be accustomed to working alone and in private. An important contribution of teacher leaders, then, is reassuring their colleagues that an examination of results with the aim of improving learning does not suggest a criticism of the work of teachers. Rather, it represents joint effort for better results.

Naturally, a focus on results and its accompanying de-privatization of practice are dependent on a school culture that honors collegial sharing of technique, an environment in which it is safe to admit questions and concerns, and an atmosphere of collaborative problem solving. It also reflects a vision of student learning in which it is not sufficient for some students to excel while others flounder or receive an inadequate education. The culture of professional inquiry reflects the collaborative nature of the effort; the strong flashlight of analysis that shines into all the school's corners does not permit teachers to hide behind claims of academic freedom. Because the culture of inquiry is a supportive one, all teachers recognize that the challenge of low achievement by some students presents a challenge for them all to take on. Furthermore, a culture of respect pervades all the discussions.

Defining Results

In their concern for results, teachers and teacher leaders are creative about how to define results and what counts as evidence of student learning. Of course, all this takes place within a larger policy environment. Government agencies also insist on results. Generally speaking, the results demanded by governments consist of scores of a certain level on standardized tests comprising machine-scorable, multiple-choice questions. Only the sort of learning that can be assessed in this manner is included on the test (such as knowledge of facts and simple procedures, with few excursions into conceptual understanding, thinking skills, or communication skills). If there are high-stakes tests, with serious consequences for either students or schools, educators feel compelled to narrow their instruction to those categories of learning.

In their quest to improve results for students, teachers have many more options within the school. The outcomes chosen by educators (and the public, for that matter) are different when the evidence for those results is not limited by the capabilities of standardized tests. Therefore, when educators want to include complex learning (such as writing, problem solving, and recognizing patterns) in their programs, they must seek other evidence of learning. This typically includes samples of student work or performance tasks. To determine the effectiveness of their work, teachers can listen to student questions, watch students' body language, analyze student writing, and examine the results of daily quizzes. And when documentation of such complex learning is required, student performance, for example in writing, can be captured and assessed against a rubric, and the results reported as numbers.

Teacher leaders, of course, play a critical role in focusing the attention of colleagues on evidence of student learning. Perhaps most important, they have expertise about the subjects they teach that permits them to know what questions to ask of the data. For example, if a group of students is experiencing difficulty learning to extrapolate information from a graph, teachers might inquire whether those students are aware of the different types of information that are best displayed on a line graph as distinct from a bar graph. Such a question permits teachers to design methods to seek the answer.

Furthermore, teacher leaders, in using their skills of persuasion, convince their colleagues of the importance of pursuing the questions, finding the data, and devising, if necessary, ways to collect pertinent information. Through their skill in facilitation, they ensure that their colleagues feel in no way attacked, that they perceive the examination of evidence as a necessary professional activity, and that all teachers, as members of the profession, are committed to improving the school's results with students.

Good information is the key to improving practice. By focusing on results, educators ensure that their efforts are targeted in the areas of greatest need. Such a focus on results should not be construed as implied criticism; instead, it is an essential component of a commitment to continuous improvement. Teacher leaders help maintain the vision and ensure that they and their colleagues keep their collective eye on the ball of enhanced student learning. Furthermore, when educators obtain better results and student performance improves, the data will reflect that trend. Hence, a focus on results serves both to point to areas in need of improvement and as the basis for encouragement and even celebration. Figure 6.1 identifies examples of practice in the area of focusing on results.

Curriculum

A school's curriculum is its public statement regarding what students who attend the school will learn. It is not the list of materials or experiences, such as *Hamlet* or a trip to the environmental education center. Rather, it states in unambiguous terms what students

	FIGURE 6.1
	Focusing on Results: Examples of Practice

Emerging teacher leaders make instructional decisions in their own teaching based on data and specific evidence within their own classes. For example, they might

- Determine the best data to help them know where their results with students could be improved.
- Collect and analyze information from their own teaching to identify patterns.
- Serve on a schoolwide committee to analyze student achievement data.

Setting	Established Teacher Leaders
Within Department or Team	Teacher leaders take the initiative within their own departments or teams to focus on results. For example, they might • Present information from their own teaching to others and encourage colleagues to collect similar information. • Pool information from different classes to determine whether there are systematic patterns regarding student learning. • Devise innovative approaches to collecting evidence of student learning.
Across the School	Teacher leaders take initiative to establish a focus on results across the school. For example, they might • Coordinate a schoolwide effort to analyze complex learning consistently across the school. • Organize a schoolwide committee to analyze student achievement data. • Design innovative approaches to find information needed for a school improvement effort.
Beyond the School	Teacher leaders participate in district, state, or national networks to focus on the results of school programs. For example, they might • Participate on a district committee to analyze district data. • Testify before policy bodies (legislatures, school board) to expand their view of meaningful evidence of student learning.

will learn from their study of *Hamlet* or their trip to the center. To that extent, the curriculum is written in the form of outcomes, statements of intended student learning.

A well-designed curriculum has several pertinent characteristics. To the extent that these are not fully developed, a school faculty might concentrate at least some of its efforts in these areas.

Publicly Known and Consistent

A good curriculum is one that is written and publicly available. Students and their parents know in advance what students will be expected to learn in any course of study. Hence, the outcomes for 5th grade mathematics or 11th grade English are available to any member of the extended school community to examine. The Internet has made the diffusion of such information far more efficient than was possible previously.

Of course, not all 5th grade students will be equally able to learn everything in the published curriculum; some may still be completing their understanding of material in the 4th grade curriculum, while others are ready to begin work on 6th grade concepts. The mechanics of how such differentiation can be accomplished is a matter of the school's or instructional team's structures for scheduling and assignment, or the instructional skills of each teacher, the focus of other sections of this book.

From a curriculum standpoint, the public nature of the curriculum is essential. Equally important is its consistency across a team or department, across a school, and across an entire district. The Algebra I curriculum is not privately held in the mind of each algebra teacher; it is not idiosyncratic to each of them. Rather, the expectations are consistent for anyone teaching the course. This is not to say that the curriculum is externally mandated by the state or any other outside body. Far from being external, the curriculum outcomes are typically the product of a school's or district's own teachers working together.

High-Level Learning

A school's curriculum should be worth learning. It should not represent the lowest common denominator of what students should learn. This provision of high-level learning is not as easy to achieve as it might sound. The practical implication of it is that when given a choice between rote learning of facts and conceptual understanding, those designing the curriculum will opt for the conceptual understanding. It also suggests, where possible, the understanding of topics in depth rather than superficial exposure to a larger number of topics.

The curriculum outcomes should represent the big ideas of each subject and should reflect the structure of the discipline. Therefore, in elementary mathematics, students not only learn how to perform certain algorithms, they understand why the algorithms work (and can derive them themselves); they understand the bigger concept of pattern and how it is manifested through different mathematics topics; they understand the concept of place value and can perform operations flexibly in any base; and they appreciate the connections between various mathematical concepts (for example, area and perimeter). Such an approach to curriculum is not reserved for the most capable students; rather, it is well within the grasp of all students and indeed may motivate them in ways that a trivial treatment of content cannot.

State and District Content Standards

At the very least, a school's curriculum must include the content that has been identified (and will be assessed) in a state's or district's curriculum framework. This is not optional. One hopes that such frameworks represent important and reasonable learning and that it is possible for students to acquire adequate knowledge and skill to perform well.

Typically, a state's or district's content standards are silent on the manner in which students should be taught the standards. Although student knowledge of content standards is likely to be assessed using a standardized test, the temptation to teach only low-level facts and skills is overcome by educators who know that approach is short-sighted and counterproductive. That is, those students who are exposed to deeper conceptual learning perform better on standardized tests than those who have experienced only superficial exposure to the content.

Balance of Outcomes

Many of the important outcomes included in the curriculum, such as those listed above, reflect knowledge and understanding. Such outcomes are essential; a school cannot claim to produce well-educated graduates unless the curriculum includes a significant amount of factual, conceptual, and procedural knowledge and understanding. Here are other important types of outcomes:

Thinking and reasoning skills. Every compilation of valued learning outcomes for students includes attention to thinking and reasoning: discerning the difference between fact and opinion, collecting and analyzing information, formulating and testing hypotheses, and predicting outcomes. These reasoning skills may be developed in any area of the curriculum and indeed can serve as unifying principles.

Communication skills. One of the most frequently heard complaints from university faculty and employers is that recent graduates possess inadequate communication skills in both speaking and writing. With the use of e-mail so pervasive, the lack of these skills is on daily display in many workplaces. There is no substitute for clear talking and writing; frequently the presence or absence of such communication skills is a reflection of the presence or absence of clear thinking. And as with thinking and reasoning, attention to communication need not be restricted to a single part of the curriculum (typically English and language arts); instead, these are skills that can and should be developed throughout the school day and in all disciplines.

Social skills. The ability to work well with colleagues is an essential skill in virtually all workplaces, as well as vital for personal fulfillment. In fact, for many years, employers have reported that when workers are dismissed, the cause relates less to technical skill than to the ability to get along with others (SCANS, 1991). Thus many teachers include in their desired outcomes the skills of collaboration. The opportunity to develop these skills is one reason teachers use instructional strategies such as cooperative learning in their classes. The skills of group work—active listening, respecting others' views, dividing work fairly and assigning roles, planning work and monitoring its completion, and assisting others—can be actively taught.

Aesthetics, disposition, and ethics. While most of the outcomes of schooling are assumed to lie in the realm of the acquisition of knowledge and skills, including social skills and thinking skills, many schools make a deliberate effort to broaden their goals to include other areas. For example, the English curriculum may include not only the skill of analyzing a novel's plot structure but the ability to appreciate the author's use of imagery. Likewise, in their treatment of the settlement of the U.S. West, many schools include the perspectives of native inhabitants, to whom settlement appeared more as an invasion. Treatments of topics of civics and analyses of historical events include attention to fundamental U.S. values such as fairness and justice, and equal rights. And most schools work to instill the habits of perseverance and open-mindedness in their students. None of these areas is likely to be included on a formal test, but all are important to a school's success in achieving its broadest aims and to students' success in life.

Coordination and Integration

Some of the most powerful learning experiences available to students arise when teachers are able to make connections between areas of the curriculum that might otherwise be regarded as separate and isolated. For instance, the history of scientific ideas enriches both social studies and science. Integrating history and literature at the secondary level is powerful: History provides a context for the literature, while literature provides a different window on historical events.

Some instructional teams, typically at the elementary level, may select a theme (rivers) for the year and organize much of their program around that concept. In these cases, the students read literature inspired by rivers, explore ancient and modern civilizations settled on rivers, and engage in mathematical and scientific explorations within the context of rivers. Naturally, the students study other topics, but the single, overarching theme unifies the curriculum in a way not possible otherwise.

A high-quality curriculum is an essential component of a school's instructional program. To a large extent, it defines student experience in the school. Therefore, it is essential that it reflect powerful learning and that opportunities be seized to make the best use of limited instructional time to offer as rich a program as possible. The role of teacher leaders is critical in making this vision a reality. They offer a broad view, they have specific expertise, and their colleagues look to them for guidance. Teacher leaders are connected with colleagues from their professional organizations; they participate in state and national conferences and are in a position to bring back insights to enrich the school's offerings. Figure 6.2 identifies ways teacher leaders can have an impact on the area of curriculum.

Student Assessment

It is virtually impossible to think about student assessment without relating it to the curriculum. Assessment, whether formative or summative, provides evidence of student learning. Indeed, it is frequently in specifying how they would know whether students have adequately achieved learning outcomes (an assessment question) that educators become really clear about what those outcomes are. That is, a curriculum statement in the mathematics curriculum that students can "solve two-step problems" is more meaningful when translated to a specific task: "Students will be able to solve problems like the following: . . ." It is the assessment task, in other words, that brings the words in the curriculum statement to life.

But not all assessment reflects broad curricular outcomes; some is more informal and is conducted within the confines of each classroom. That is, while some assessment is summative, conveying the degree of student learning of the school's or district's curriculum, other assessment is formative, used on a daily basis by both teachers and students to guide learning (Wiggins, 1993).

In order for assessment to serve a positive purpose in a school's program, the school must embrace a culture of hard work and success as described in Chapter 4. Unless both

	FIGURE 6.2
	Curriculum: Examples of Practice

Emerging teacher leaders examine and deepen the curriculum within their own classes. For example, they might

- Work to deepen the content they teach.
- Integrate topics from different areas of the curriculum.

Setting	Established Teacher Leaders
Within Department or Team	Teacher leaders initiate projects with colleagues within their own departments or teams to analyze and improve their curriculum. For example, they might • Organize an effort to ensure that the curriculum is consistent among all members of the team or department. • Explore ways to integrate the different subjects they teach. • Work to deepen the curriculum and make it more rigorous. • Ensure that the curriculum includes an appropriate balance of different types of outcomes.
Across the School	Teacher leaders take the initiative to improve the curriculum across the school. For example, they might • Analyze the school's curriculum against the state or district content standards. • Ensure that the curriculum represents important learning in the different disciplines. • Work to ensure consistency of the curriculum across the school. • Participate in a district curriculum mapping effort.
Beyond the School	Teacher leaders participate in district, state, or national networks for curriculum improvement. For example, they might • Participate in a district curriculum revision effort. • Serve on a state standards committee. • Serve on a textbook adoption committee.

teachers and students are committed to high-level learning and are willing to work to achieve it, the information derived from assessment (whether summative or formative) will not result in action. That is, assessment results yield information as to what has not yet been mastered. This information is essential both to teachers in planning next steps and to students in focusing their efforts. But if neither teachers nor students are committed to hard work and success, they will not use the information to maximize learning.

Rather, students will try to "game" the system (achieving high grades whether or not they are deserved) and teachers will use the assessment results only to enter marks in the grade book.

Summative Assessment

Consistency of curriculum outcomes across a school or district typically involves consensus on summative assessments, usually end-of-course or end-of-semester exams. It is through this consistency of assessment that the school or district can be sure that Algebra I, for example, is the same course regardless of the teacher in charge. That is not to say that teachers don't, from time to time, introduce a favorite topic that might not be part of the official curriculum, but all students (and their parents) are assured that they are receiving at least the standard curriculum.

It should be noted that external assessments can have, paradoxically, a positive effect on student-teacher relationships. When the only tests that students take have been designed by the teacher (either alone or in collaboration with colleagues), students feel, with some justification, that they are being judged by their teacher. Therefore, the relationship between them is somewhat adversarial. On the other hand, when students are preparing for a test developed by an external agency (whether the state or the College Board for Advanced Placement courses), the teacher and the students are partners. That is, the teacher and students are, in a sense, coconspirators in helping the students do well on the assessment. This change in emphasis can have an important effect on their interaction.

Summative assessments may be of several different types and frequently comprise a combination of different methodologies. They may include what measurement experts call "select" items, meaning that students select a response from those provided. The best example of this assessment is the type of multiple-choice or true/false test that many students are familiar with. Or a test can include or consist entirely of constructed response items, in which students write a response (for example, a short answer or an essay).

All tests are administered under what educators know as testing conditions. Students have limited time and typically no access to each other or to materials as they do their work. This is in contrast to other assessment methods, in which students complete work at home (such as a paper or a project) that is then assessed against clear criteria using a scoring guide or rubric. Similarly, an assessment may take the form of a product (for example, a painting in an art class) through which students demonstrate their understanding and skill. Lastly, assessment can take the form of a performance, as when students give a speech or a report in class or read a passage in a language they are studying as an assessment of their pronunciation.

Summative assessments, in order to be valid tests of student understanding, must include certain characteristics:

Appropriateness to the curriculum. It is essential that summative assessments of student learning be aligned to the curricular outcomes. It does not make sense to assess student skill in writing by asking students to take a test of grammar; likewise, the only way to assess mathematical problem-solving skills is to ask students to solve problems, not perform routine operations.

Suitability to diverse learners. Not all students are good test takers. Although it is important for students to become as skilled as possible in taking tests, such a skill is fundamentally irrelevant to educators' knowledge as to whether the students have learned the curriculum. Furthermore, some students have difficulty writing rapidly; they should not be put at a disadvantage by the assessment methodologies selected.

Clear standards of performance. Educators must make clear to students how their work will be assessed. If students are writing an essay, for example, what are the criteria by which it will be judged? Do the organization and structure matter? What about the richness of the vocabulary? Or the quality of examples? If any or all of these criteria are important, they should be specified and made known to students. Furthermore, it is not only the evaluative criteria that should be clarified, but also the expected level of performance as laid out in a scoring guide or rubric. Indeed, many teachers have discovered that developing the scoring guides with students enhances the students' understanding of what they are learning with no sacrifice in the rigor of the assessment.

Multiple measures and methodologies. It is a fundamental principle of assessment that no one assessment event should carry undue weight; everyone, including a student, has a bad day from time to time. The goal of summative assessment, after all, is to determine whether students have learned the curriculum. Occasionally it makes sense to have a test count for a large percentage of a grade, but students should not have their entire grade for a course—or even a significant portion of it—rest on the outcome of a single event. Not only does it put tremendous strain on students, it is likely to permit the assessment of only a portion of the important outcomes of the course.

Formative Assessment

Not all educational assessment takes place in formal settings as a test or major project. Every day in class, teachers engage in formative assessment of their students. This is an integral part of teaching; most teachers do it without even thinking of it as assessment (Lewin & Shoemaker, 1998; Mitchell, 1992; Stiggins, 1994).

It is important to be clear as to how formative assessment differs from summative assessment. Both are aligned to the curriculum and provide evidence of the degree of student learning. But formative assessment is purely for the purpose of student learning; there are no consequences for students' grades or class standing. Teachers use formative assessment to provide timely, individual feedback to students. Students can monitor their own learning and ascertain where they need to work harder. In other words, formative assessment is assessment, but it does not affect the final grade; it is part of the instructional process and contributes to learning.

The skillful use of formative assessment is central to a teacher's ability to differentiate instruction. When a teacher is alert to signals, or deliberately elicits them, students provide ample indicators of their degree of understanding. By acting on this information, teachers individualize their teaching and demonstrate their commitment to each student.

Some of the techniques teachers use to conduct formative assessment include the following:

• *Homework.* Student success in completing homework can provide, to both students and their teachers, important information as to what has been mastered and what needs more work.

• *Daily quizzes.* Like homework, frequent quizzes provide evidence of student learning.

• *Student questions.* During class, students reveal the extent of their understanding through the questions they ask and the comments they make during class discussions.

• *Student class work.* Some students reveal that they "get it" or not through their participation, or lack of it, in learning activities. When teachers are able to monitor students working during class, they can gather important information as to the degree of student understanding.

The degree to which formative assessment can support effective student learning relates, as does much else, to the school's culture. When both teachers and students are committed to high-level learning, and when the school has instituted a culture of hard work and success, then students themselves appreciate the value of formative assessment in guiding their learning. That is, they recognize that one purpose of homework is to test their understanding (not just busywork mandated by the teacher) so they can concentrate on those areas needing more work. Similarly, their questions in class are not to show off their intelligence but to clarify points they don't yet understand. Formative assessment, in other words, is purposeful for both teacher and students.

Assessment is an essential part of the effort of teaching and learning. It takes many forms, with varying degrees of student involvement. However, many teachers have not received extensive preparation in this area and can therefore benefit from a focus on assessment techniques, both summative and formative. At the same time, other teachers have deep experience in this area; their expertise can be tapped for the benefit of everyone. Teacher leaders are alert to these opportunities to improve teaching and learning in their teams or departments, across the school, and beyond the school.

There are many different aspects to classroom assessment. Given the uneven preparation of teachers in this area, it is a fruitful focus for sustained work by study groups. Unfortunately, because of their weak preparation, some teachers may be reluctant to take it on; they may not want to appear inadequate in front of their colleagues. The role of teacher leaders in offering reassurance and support can be a critical one. Figure 6.3 presents ways that teacher leaders can play a role in student assessment.

Teaching

The quality of teaching is the most important factor that influences student learning. Other components, of course, play a role, from the quality of the curriculum to the policies and programs for students. But it is in the quality of instruction where all the elements come together in an alchemy that students remember for years. Therefore, no matter what else educational leaders (whether teacher leaders or administrators) do, they must not neglect the skill of teachers in this core responsibility.

Standards of Practice

In promoting improved instruction, clear standards of practice are essential. There are many sets of standards that can be used; each has been developed for different purposes,

FIGURE 6.3

Student Assessment: Examples of Practice

Emerging teacher leaders improve their skills in assessment within their own classes. For example, they might

- Enlist the help of their students in developing a new scoring rubric.
- Refine their procedures for formative assessment.
- Utilize a range of types of assessment evidence in gauging the learning of their own students.

Setting	Established Teacher Leaders
Within Department or Team	Teacher leaders engage their colleagues within their own departments or teams in a consideration of assessment. For example, they might • Coordinate the development of a consistent end-of-course test for use across the department. • Initiate a project to develop a single rubric for assessing student work throughout the department or team. • Mobilize the efforts of teachers to share their procedures for formative assessment.
Across the School	Teacher leaders take the initiative to improve assessment practices across the school. For example, they might • Arrange for a workshop on rubric development for the entire school. • Organize a review for all teachers on the techniques of formative assessment. • Coordinate the design of a schoolwide approach to the assessment of, for example, writing.
Beyond the School	Teacher leaders participate in district, state, or national networks for the improvement of assessment practices. For example, they might • Contribute to an initiative to develop districtwide summative assessments. • Make a presentation at a state or local conference on alternative methods of assessment. • Serve on a statewide committee designing a handbook for teachers on the use of assessment methodologies in their classrooms.

and all have their strengths and limitations. Educators learned many years ago from Madeline Hunter (1978, 1982) the value of a common language to describe teaching in order to permit meaningful professional conversation. Although the profession has advanced since Hunter's initial efforts, the essential finding remains valid: Clear standards of practice contribute to the professionalism of teaching by permitting reflection on practice and purposeful dialogue.

Many states have promulgated teaching standards, and these vary in their level of detail. Typically, however, they consist of 5 to 10 broad statements of what is good teaching, sometimes with more specific indicators listed for each one. As a guide for the expectations of education programs in preparing new teachers, the Interstate New Teacher Assessment and Support Consortium (INTASC, 1992), an outgrowth of the Council of Chief State School Officers, published 10 principles, each with knowledge, performances, and dispositions intended to further elaborate on them. These principles have been widely adopted by universities designing teacher preparation programs and by some states to define good teaching. In addition, the National Board for Professional Teaching Standards (1989) has described five core principles and then has developed more detailed teaching standards based on those principles for each of more than 30 teaching specialties (for example, early childhood, middle-level mathematics). These standards and their accompanying assessments are designed to describe the work of experienced and highly accomplished teachers. The assessment process is rigorous and is regarded by most teachers who complete it to be professionally valuable.

Characteristics of Good Standards of Practice

Standards of professional practice for educators consist of far more than a random listing of desirable skills and dispositions. When policymakers and practitioners set out to write standards, they find that the best are those that share certain characteristics. Specifically, the best standards

• *Are valid.* Standards of practice should be valid, reflecting both research evidence and the "wisdom of practice" of practitioners.

• *Are clear and unambiguous.* Standards of practice should be written in clear, sensible language, rather than educational or research jargon.

• *Are organized in a coherent structure, with each level defining the one above.* If the standards are organized in a hierarchical structure, with, for example, six main standards followed by smaller elements of each one, those elements should serve to define the full meaning of the broader standard. Important ideas, in other words, should not be left out.

• *Are of roughly equal size.* Standards of practice are of greatest value if they have divided the work of teaching into various components of approximately equal size, or heft. This permits better analysis of practice.

• *Reflect teaching skills for important student learning.* If the aims of education include conceptual understanding of complex content and skills of reasoning and argumentation in addition to low-level knowledge, then the skills of teachers must be correspondingly rich and sophisticated.

• *Contain descriptive narrative.* It is not sufficient to simply list the work of teaching in bulleted points, even when the hierarchical structure provides extensive examples of indicators. If one takes the view that teaching is complex work, then the list must be accompanied by at least brief narrative descriptions of the meanings of the different standards.

• *Contain rubrics reflecting levels of performance.* If standards of practice are to be used to promote professional conversation, then it is important to be able to recognize the extent to which they are being accomplished well, or partially; rubrics provide that information. Only then can teachers determine where they should focus their efforts to be most productive.

• *Are nonprescriptive.* Standards of practice should not specify a particular style or methodology of teaching, but should be written in such a manner that they allow many approaches to teaching.

• *Are nonredundant.* Each standard should encompass a single important idea, with clear delineations between the different standards, to the extent possible. And if smaller components are listed for each of the standards, they should be properly situated. This is more easily accomplished if the standards themselves are not redundant.

• *Permit "downstream" uses.* Occasionally standards of practice are devised and then used for a purpose that was not predicted by the original developers and for which they are poorly suited. Therefore, the purposes of standards of practice should be identified before they are written, to the extent possible; this will save much difficulty later, including completely rewriting them. In particular, if standards are to be used for assessment (either formative or summative), it should be clear from the manner in which they are written what would count as evidence of practice.

The Framework for Teaching

Another nationally used set of standards to describe good teaching comes from *Enhancing Professional Practice: A Framework for Teaching* (Danielson, 1996). It has been adopted by many school districts and several states (sometimes after some modification) as their definition of teaching. The framework for teaching divides the complex work of teaching into the four broad areas.

Domain 1: Planning and preparation. Comprising six smaller components, planning and preparation includes the work of teachers as they solidify their understanding of the content they teach and come to know their students. It includes being clear about one's instructional goals, knowing the available resources, and designing both the instruction and the approach to assessment. Planning and preparation is essential to good teaching: simply put, good teachers plan well. However, the converse is not necessarily true. Just because a teacher plans well, it does not mean that the actual instruction will go well. Planning and preparation, then, is essential behind-the-scenes work of teaching and is a necessary but not sufficient condition for good instruction.

Domain 2: The classroom environment. Domain 2 deals with the physical and interpersonal environment and contains five smaller components. These include such things as the quality of interactions (both between teacher and students and among students), the culture of the class for learning, routines and procedures, standards of conduct, and use of physical space. The classroom environment is that part of teaching that most educators, as they are beginning their practice, find they must master before good instruction is possible; the classroom must be orderly, students must know the expectations and routines, and there must be a safe and welcoming atmosphere. When adults recall their school experiences years later, it is aspects of Domain 2 that they tend to recall most vividly.

Domain 3: Instruction. Domain 3 is the heart of teaching; it is where teachers bring the content to life for their students. Divided into five smaller components, Domain 3 includes clarity of communication, use of questioning and discussion techniques, engagement of students in learning, use of assessment for instruction, and flexibility and responsiveness. Taken together, these components describe the complex interaction of students and teacher in engaging with important content. While the other domains of teaching are essential, they are, in effect, important only insofar as they support Domain 3. That is, it is for the purpose of student engagement in learning that teachers plan, prepare, and establish a supportive and orderly environment.

Domain 4: Professional responsibilities. Not all teaching takes place in, or is even directly supportive of, the daily work of classroom practice. Domain 4 describes those aspects of teaching that are important to skilled teaching but are not connected to instruction on any given day or for a single instructional unit. Instead, Domain 4, divided into six smaller components, concerns general professional skills such as reflection on practice, maintaining records, communicating with families, and the like. The skills of Domain 4 have only recently been recognized as critical to excellent teaching. However, the research on teacher reflection, for example, is compelling; skill in reflection is essential to good practice.

Promoting Improved Practice

It is difficult to overstate the importance of teaching in enhancing student learning. Therefore, the efforts of teacher leaders, such as those in Figure 6.4, are critical. Unfortunately, many teachers are threatened by a close examination of practice because they assume an implied criticism.

In this light, it is instructive to consider the manner in which Japanese lesson study is conducted. In that approach to instructional improvement, developed in Japan but now used around the world, a team of teachers jointly plans a lesson. A member of the team then teaches the lesson to her students while the others observe. Following the lesson, the team reconvenes to analyze the lesson and determine how it can be improved. The next version is then taught by another member of the team to another group of students. The process continues as long as is needed (or as long as is possible, given the population of the school or grade level). The lesson study process is described by Catherine Lewis (2002). The important aspect of this approach, however, is that the focus of the teachers is on *the lesson,* not on the performance of individual teachers. That is, the discussions are about the lesson and whether it worked, not about whether a teacher taught well. This is a critical distinction, one that alters the tone of professional conversations. In this environment, teachers are jointly engaged in a search for the best approach, not critiquing one another.

In addition, many schools have implemented Cognitive Coaching (Costa & Garmston, 1994), a technique by which educators (typically teachers, but it could involve administrators) assist one another in a nonjudgmental manner to improve their teaching. In this approach, the agenda for the interaction is set by the teacher; the coach's role is purely one of assisting the teacher in what that teacher wants to improve. When well used, this strategy is nonthreatening and is a vehicle for enhanced reflection and professional conversation.

FIGURE 6.4		
Teaching: Examples of Practice		
Emerging teacher leaders work within their own classes to improve their teaching. For example, they might		
• Conduct a self-assessment of practice and identify areas that could be strengthened.		
• Determine which aspects of teaching are most important in their own setting.		
• Serve as a mentor for a new teacher.		
• Have a student teacher in their own class.		

Setting	Established Teacher Leaders
Within Department or Team	Teacher leaders initiate conversations about the quality of teaching within their own departments or teams. For example, they might • Initiate a study group with their colleagues to conduct self-assessments of practice. • Organize a Japanese lesson study to examine the team's or department's approach to a certain topic or concept. • Train colleagues to serve as mentors. • Organize the student teachers who will be assigned to the team or department.
Across the School	Teacher leaders organize efforts to enhance teaching across the school. For example, they might • Implement a procedure by which teachers are able to observe one another's classrooms to obtain ideas they could use. • Structure a mentoring program for the school. • Serve as the student-teacher coordinator for the school. • Become certified as a trainer for a new instructional approach and offer workshops for colleagues.
Beyond the School	Teacher leaders participate in district, state, or national networks for improving the quality of teaching. For example, they might • Design a mentoring program for the district. • Serve as the student teacher liaison for the district. • Teach a class for prospective teachers through a local university. • Serve as an officer for a professional organization.

◇◇◇◇◇◇◇◇◇◇◇◇◇◇◇◇◇

Teaching and learning is at the heart of the school's mission, and the quality of teaching is at the core of teaching and learning. Teaching is where norms of privacy are most entrenched and, in some school cultures, most vigorously defended. Issues of privacy constitute the challenge for teacher leaders who wish to serve as a catalyst for improved practice.

7

Communications and Community Relations

Not all the work of schools takes place within the four walls of the building. Schools are members of their communities, and as such, they participate in the broader web of other educational institutions, agencies, the corporate world, and of course, the parents of their students. Through both formal and informal structures, educators establish and maintain connections with the broader community; teacher leaders play an important role in these networks.

Family Communication and Involvement

Educators recognize the importance of family participation in the education of children. This is not an insignificant matter; while there are some students who can overcome ignorance, indifference, or outright hostility to their academic ambitions at home, successful students, in the main, have the support of involved families.

Much of the responsibility for family communication rests with individual teachers in their interactions with the parents of students they teach. This important aspect of teaching is a central component of Domain 4 of the Framework for Teaching described in Chapter 6. Individual teachers keep the parents of their students informed about the instructional program as a whole and about the progress of their children. In addition, teachers incorporate students' home lives, where appropriate, into the ways they present material. For example, they might invite students to learn about the decade of the 1960s from the experiences of their parents or grandparents and to share those stories in class.

Teachers use many techniques to engage with parents. Some of these are formal: a handout for back-to-school night, instructions on what students should wear for a field trip, or a weekly newsletter. In addition, teachers make contact with parents of individual students about concerns regarding the students' progress, either academically or socially. This is institutionalized in parent-teacher conferences and may be supplemented by more frequent communications, such as phone calls, notes, and e-mail messages.

Communication with families is part of the work of teaching that is done by all teachers in the course of their day-to-day tasks. Teacher leaders can contribute to the effectiveness of their colleagues by, for example, offering their weekly newsletter as a template for others to use. But in general, communication with the families of the students one teaches is part of every teacher's responsibility.

In addition, educators establish and maintain broader team or schoolwide communication with families of students, and in these efforts teacher leaders play a pivotal role. This communication might be initiated and conducted by a single team or department with a focus on that level or subject, or it could engage teachers from the entire school, with participation from across the student population. These programs generally serve one of several purposes, which are described below.

Information About the School's Programs (Instructional and Noninstructional)

Many schools take pride in their offerings and look for opportunities to convey information to families about those offerings. They may want to spread the word about a new program, such as an improved approach to teaching reading or science, or simply explain existing programs, such as the school's approach to discipline infractions, or course offerings and the guidance program at a high school. Some of this information can be conveyed in writing, perhaps in the school's handbook, while some is best presented in person in an informational or workshop setting. Furthermore, many schools and districts have created Web sites where parents can obtain information about academics, activities, and sports.

Some schools have instituted student-led conferences, in which students show their parents what they have been learning and participate in a three-way discussion with the teacher. Such an approach is effective because it engages students directly in self-assessment and reflection on their own learning, sending a powerful message about the nature of partnership. But student-led conferences are most effective when they represent the practice of not only a single teacher but a whole department or team or, better yet, an entire school.

Whenever parents are invited to the school, for any purpose, it is often helpful to provide child care for younger siblings. This can make the difference for some parents as to whether they can attend; even when they don't personally take advantage of the service, parents recognize that it respects the complicated lives that many parents lead.

Opportunities abound for teacher leaders to play an important role in the school's outreach to parents. They might organize a math night to explain (possibly in a workshop setting) the school's or district's approach to teaching mathematics. They could offer to revise their department's description in the school handbook. Teacher leaders might help parents understand the test results that are sent from the state. They might coordinate the school's schedule for student-led conferences, preparing the information to be sent to parents about the approach.

Information About Child and Adolescent Development

Most parents are not experts in child and adolescent development; simply having children does not automatically convey such insight. Therefore, the school can play an important role in helping parents better understand the academic and social development of young people. An incidental benefit of such offerings is that the parents may make better choices with respect to their younger children than they would have without such information.

Information about child and adolescent development can take many forms. It might be a regular column in the school's or district's newsletter or a series of workshops with a member of the staff who is knowledgeable about cognitive or social development. Many parents are astonished to learn, for example, that their 1st grade children may not have developed a stable understanding of the concept of number (and the implications of this for their learning of mathematics), or that 6th graders are still acquiring the concept of proportional reasoning (with implications for studying algebra). Similarly, children's social and moral reasoning develop throughout elementary school; parents can promote this development if they understand it.

Parents of adolescents are keenly interested in knowing what makes their children tick and how they can help them make good choices. Many parents don't understand why it is that some students get in with the wrong crowd or experiment with dangerous drugs. This information is important to parents as their children mature; the school's policies regarding drug use, for example, are important, but if parents have an understanding of their children's development, they can better support the students and prevent problems.

Supporting Student Learning

Parents are a child's first teachers, and they continue to play a role throughout childhood and adolescence. Of course, that role evolves over time as the children themselves gradually distance themselves from the orbit of their immediate families. Throughout their school years, however, families exert influence and support of their children's learning to some extent.

Recent research has documented the importance of engagement of families in their children's learning (Fantuzzo, McWayne, Perry, & Childs, 2004). This support can take many forms: providing children with a learning space at home, asking them about their school day, reading aloud, and generally taking an interest in their learning. Even a small, dedicated space with good light and some degree of privacy can make a difference. So can reasonable rules about television watching or talking with friends until the homework is completed. In some families, where the parents' schedules are grueling, older children are needed to help in the household to care for younger siblings or to prepare an evening meal. If homework is to be an important part of the instructional program, some parents may need assistance in supporting their children in completing it.

Many parents have not given thought to how they might support their children's learning, short of being able to offer substantive tutoring assistance. They may not be aware of how small actions such as a routine of daily bedtime reading can contribute to learning. The school can play an important role in providing suggestions to families regarding their unique role in education and how they can make it more likely that the children will complete homework on time.

Other support for parents may be more substantive in an academic sense. Parents sometimes become deeply involved in their children's schoolwork by assisting with homework or helping to organize a science project. The latter situation raises important ethical issues; in some schools, students complete such projects in school, using only material that is available—and available to all students—in school. This ensures that all students have an equal opportunity to excel.

Without the ethical issues of parent overinvolvement in school projects, it is important that teachers not assume that parents are available to assist their children in completing assignments, since such assistance is much more readily available in some households (typically those where the parents are themselves well educated) than in others. Schools seriously committed to high-level learning by all students ensure access to after-hours assistance for everyone.

Many parents are genuinely baffled by what their children are learning in school and would like to understand it better themselves. Therefore, a "Parents' Guide to Pre-Algebra," or similar documents related to other subjects, can keep parents informed about what their children are learning and might enable them to offer assistance when it is actually needed. Furthermore, such documents can be of real value to the parents themselves if they, for example, are taking a test to qualify for a new job and need to brush up on their skills.

Educational Offerings for Parents

Every school is essentially empty for many hours of every day, from the time the students leave in the afternoon until the next morning. Yet the school contains much valuable equipment, and the staff possesses important expertise from which members of the community could benefit. Many school districts make extensive use of their facilities in the evening, providing a wide range of courses for parents and other members of the community. These range from language, science, and computer courses to courses that provide adults the opportunity to learn crafts or music. Furthermore, these community programs are typically organized and taught by individuals who may have no other connection to the school. That is, the role of teachers in the community education program may be negligible unless they have elected to teach a course.

However, because teachers are in touch with the parents of the students they teach, they may be in the best position to both elicit the interests of those parents and encourage them to take advantage of offerings in the community education program. Furthermore, some teachers may decide to offer a short, single-session introduction to subjects of interest, such as using the Internet or jazz of the 1930s. These sessions can help parents support their children's learning and are also likely to be of interest in their own lives. Being aware of such opportunities and taking the time and trouble to make them available is a mark of a truly committed professional educator.

Family Engagement (Governance and Social)

Many schools have site councils that have a spot or two specifically reserved for parents of students in the school. These councils are charged with various responsibilities and have varying degrees of actual decision-making power. Some, for example, may help to screen and hire a new principal or faculty member or approve the school's budget, while others might be more of a conduit for communication between the school and the parent community. Regardless of the specific arrangements, site councils are important to the overall governance of the school and depend on the active participation of at least a few parents.

Not all parents have the time or the inclination to serve on a site council, and some may believe that they have little to contribute. It is part of the role of leadership in the school, whether exercised by administrators or teachers, to reach out to parents and encourage them to become involved in the workings of the school. In making that outreach, educators recognize that in any school there tend to be a few parents who take every opportunity to volunteer; there is the danger that theirs will be the only parent voices heard. Broadening the representation of parents requires tact and skill.

Not all parent engagement in the school concerns the school's programs. Schools are also social institutions, and parents are part of their extended family. Therefore, some schools institute family nights with a primarily social purpose—a spaghetti dinner, for example, or a film viewing. Many of these events are organized by a parent organization (PTO/PTA), but teachers typically also serve on those bodies.

Teacher leaders play an important role in engaging parents in the life of the school. For a start, they are in contact with the parents of the students they teach, and they can encourage them to become involved more broadly. But in addition, teacher leaders are alert to the larger system of which their own department or team is a part; they have the big picture in mind. Therefore, teacher leaders are able to connect with parents of students in ways that go beyond their own teaching responsibilities and encourage parents to be involved in school events or participate in offerings. In addition, they are likely to serve on the school's site council. Figure 7.1 shows ways in which teacher leaders might engage and communicate with families in their schools.

Communication with Other Educators

As students move through a school, they encounter many different teachers. And as they move through the district and, frequently, on to postsecondary learning, they

	FIGURE 7.1
	Family Communication and Involvement: Examples of Practice

Emerging teacher leaders engage the families of the students they teach in the life of the school. For example, they might

- Prepare a document for parents explaining the major concepts their children are learning.
- Encourage the parents of their students to serve on the site council.

Setting	Established Teacher Leaders
Within Department or Team	Teacher leaders take initiative to encourage family communication and engagement within their own departments or teams. For example, they might • Present a family evening describing the team's or department's program. • Organize an outside expert to address a parent group on important developmental characteristics of the age group the team teaches. • Periodically publish a team or department newsletter for parents. • Coordinate a family event, such as a picnic, for families to get acquainted.
Across the School	Teacher leaders promote outreach efforts for parents across the school. For example, they might • Provide the leadership for collecting information for the school's Web site. • Organize schoolwide programs for parents about topics of interest to them (e.g., for example, drug prevention) regardless of the specific age of their children. • Coordinate the development of materials for parents describing the school's overall curriculum. • Design and teach a course for parents (e.g., on computer use). • Offer a workshop for parents on how to read to their child or how to make use of daily events to develop mathematical concepts. • Initiate a "Family Reading Night" in the school library, where parents and children come for an hour of reading and can borrow a book to take home.
Beyond the School	Teacher leaders participate in district, state, or national networks to engage families. For example, they might • Serve on the district or state PTA/PTO, contributing to its work. • Prepare a district curriculum document for distribution to parents. • Help prepare district or state materials for parents on topics such as how to help their children with homework or resist drugs. • Prepare a guide for parents on a subject in the curriculum that they might not understand, such as algebra.

attend many different schools and institutions. Furthermore, if families move often, students' school experience is even more fragmented than when students remain in the same district for their K–12 education. To maximize student learning, communication among educators within a school and at different levels (or in different schools at the same level, for transient students) is essential. In spite of moving to different schools, students can and should experience a certain degree of continuity in their education.

Communication Within the School

As students move through the elementary grades, they are assigned to a series of different grade-level teachers. In addition, many schools are fortunate enough to have specialty teachers in art, music, and physical education, and occasionally foreign (or world) languages. Students with special needs may participate in classes in the core subjects outside the regular classroom setting altogether. Naturally, secondary-level students learn each subject from teachers who are particularly expert in that discipline. But this also means that several different teachers interact with individual students during the course of the day and the year, and they inevitably see the students in varying lights, depending on the content of the course and the students' ability and interest in it.

Whenever many teachers work with an individual student, there are issues of communication. Each teacher sees the student in a specific setting, one in which the student may have particular gifts or limitations. In the absence of clear and well-developed methods of communication, these insights tend to be restricted to the individual teacher; however, it is in the best interest of students that such insights be shared and that systems are in place to enable that sharing. This need is particularly acute, for example, when an individual elementary student is learning to read from a classroom teacher, a reading teacher, and a special education teacher, all of whom may be assisted by a different teacher's aide or volunteer. In such situations, coordination is difficult (though essential) to achieve, and it depends first of all on good communication.

Communication with Other Schools in the District

In many districts, the degree of individual school autonomy is quite astonishing. When there is a single middle or high school, this independence is understandable. But when several schools within a district serve the same level of students, and yet do not communicate, valuable opportunities are lost for mutual understanding and professional collaboration.

Most important, when students move from one school to another (elementary to middle school, or middle to high school) they are, typically, simply attending another school in the same district. Even in districts that serve only elementary or only high school students, the feeder patterns are well established; educators know where their students are going or from where they have come.

When a new group of students arrives into a middle school from the elementary schools, for example, much information about them is typically lost. Those students' teachers have come to know them well during their elementary years, and yet the middle school teachers must begin with a clean slate. If the middle school teachers have taught older siblings of an entering student, such familiarity may actually be misleading; even children within the same family are famously different from one another. At the very least, the middle school staff can get up to speed more quickly with a group of students if they have good information about their level of performance in the basic skills and the assessments of earlier teachers in such matters as creativity, perseverance, and social skills. It is in the best interest of the students if teachers find ways to share their knowledge about individuals and groups of students; less time is lost in the transition.

In some districts, children move around within a district during the course of the year. This can reflect low income, as families must vacate an apartment when the rent is due. When students' schooling is frequently interrupted, and particularly when the children involved are the most vulnerable, educators must redouble their efforts to communicate effectively with their colleagues in other schools. A uniform district curriculum makes this easier and more efficient, of course, but the systems for sharing information must be in place and must be used.

Communication with Schools in Other Districts

It is a fact of U.S. society that many families are highly mobile. Families move across the country in response to an employment opportunity or move to another section of the same area or state when they can afford better housing. Alternatively, movement may reflect seasonal patterns, as in the case of migrant workers who follow the harvest.

Communication among educators when students move from one district to another is more challenging than when the students move within a district. Sometimes it is difficult to discover even where the students have come from or what they have learned in previous years. Schools with large numbers of transient students often devise efficient methods of intake assessment of student knowledge and skill so that as little instructional time is lost as possible. They may assign a teacher, and perhaps a teacher's assistant as well, to the specific role of determining the level of performance of new students within the first day or two of their appearance. They reason that they may not have much time with these students and that they need to make the best use of it that they can. But since all schools receive students from different locations, it is in their collective best interests to devise efficient methods of communicating information about children's prior learning.

Communication with Postsecondary Institutions

Increasing numbers of students are pursuing postsecondary education in a variety of settings: community colleges, four-year colleges and universities, and technical or vocational programs.

Many postsecondary institutions have their own procedures to screen incoming students; when students arrive from many different areas of the state, or even from other states or countries, this makes sense for them to do. But if a high school has a particularly innovative approach to teaching or uses an unconventional grading system, that staff must communicate with the admissions directors of higher learning institutions so they can make informed decisions about the students. Furthermore, high schools in an area may have ongoing and frequent contact with their local community college. By streamlining their communication strategies, the students' progress in learning can be continuous.

Communication with postsecondary institutions can and should flow two ways. It is important for postsecondary institutions to be familiar with the programs of the schools from which their new students come. It is equally important, however, for the educators in the high schools to listen carefully to instructors in the postsecondary institutions regarding patterns of strength and weakness they have found among graduates of the high schools. If a community college finds, for example, that graduates of a certain high school write particularly well or poorly, this is important information for the faculty of the high school, as it might suggest revisions they should make to their program.

Good communication among educators in a single school or district—and beyond the district—is an important concrete manifestation of the educators' belief that they are part of a broader professional community. In taking on these communication responsibilities, teachers assert the primary claim of student learning on daily practice; they know that only by being part of the larger community can they offer to students the best program of which the school is capable.

Teacher leaders take initiative in ensuring that communication is frequent and smooth. They are alert to opportunities to improve both the quantity and quality of communication among educators; they are, after all, serving the same group of students. It only makes sense for them to be aware of what everyone is doing. Figure 7.2 lists practices involved in communicating with other educators.

Partnerships with Universities, Businesses, and Community Agencies

Educators have both professional and practical reasons for entering into partnerships with other organizations in the community, including universities, businesses, and public and private agencies. These partnerships all serve one principal purpose: to improve the school's program by enhancing the skills of educators, strengthening the programs offered to students, and avoiding duplication among various organizations.

There are also informal partnerships, of course. Many teachers make it their business to know of resources in the community that can be tapped to strengthen the school's offerings for students. These include organizations such as planetariums and zoos, as well as individuals with expertise who can share their knowledge with students. And the local police, fire, and first aid squads typically include outreach to schools as part of their mission.

Teacher leaders play an important role in these links: They are the instructional experts in the community, and their views have credibility. Furthermore, because they know the students and their families, they have a broad view of the community as a whole. Simultaneously, they have a comprehensive sense of the school's and district's programs and what would serve to enrich them.

Colleges and Universities

Communication with universities regarding the instructional program and individual students has been addressed in the section on communication. The focus here is on professional collaboration with university personnel for the purpose of strengthening the school's instructional program. These collaborations are of several different types.

Student offerings. In every school district, there are a few students who have exhausted the high school's program in at least some areas of the curriculum. For

---

	FIGURE 7.2 **Communication with Other Educators: Examples of Practice**

Emerging teacher leaders develop communication devices to communicate with colleagues about their students. For example, they might

- Develop a recording sheet about their own students' strengths in group work.
- Ask the school office to obtain a new student's records from his previous school.

Setting	Established Teacher Leaders
Within Department or Team	Teacher leaders coordinate efforts for professional communication within their own departments or teams. For example, they might • Establish and maintain a team or departmentwide system for student mastery of sections of the curriculum. • Initiate a regular meeting time with colleagues for conferring about individual students.
Across the School	Teacher leaders take the initiative to strengthen communication with educators across the school and on behalf of the school with external institutions. For example, they might • Develop procedures for specialist and generalist teachers to share their assessments of and plans for individual students. • Coordinate the development of a schoolwide process for monitoring students' progress as they move from one grade to another. • Establish procedures for all teachers who have worked with an individual student over several years to share their insights, contributing to better planning for that student.
Beyond the School	Teacher leaders participate in district, state, or national networks for intradistrict communication. For example, they might • Get together with educators from other districts to share methods for collecting and sharing information about students when they move from one district to another. • Coordinate with other districts an orientation session for local institutions of higher education to explain the various programs and grading systems. • Coordinate the development of procedures and forms to communicate with educators within the district but at other levels. • Take the initiative to formulate methods for students who leave the district to carry information with them about their learning.

example, a student may be ready for advanced work in a world language or in mathematics. These students may have already taken every course offered in the high school by their junior year, and yet don't have sufficient overall credits to graduate. In these cases, students may be able to take a course or two at a local college, particularly if they have exhausted not only the course offerings of the high school but the expertise of the teachers. Scheduling and transportation are practical difficulties that must be worked out, but the concept is clear: to offer courses of sufficient rigor to challenge all students throughout their high school careers.

Professional offerings. Many teachers are able to take advantage of the proximity of a local college or university to enrich their own academic knowledge. This may be directly connected with their teaching responsibilities (as when a social studies teacher takes a course in Chinese history) or for the purpose of general broadening of expertise In either case, teachers are able to extend their knowledge and hence be more effective with their own students.

In addition, a local university may offer professional courses through which teachers can extend their instructional skill. For example, courses in cooperative learning or discipline-specific pedagogy will almost certainly contribute to a teacher's repertoire of strategies that can be used in the classroom. Such courses not only build a teacher's professional skill, they are almost certainly eligible to satisfy the state's requirements for relicensure or qualify for movement on a district's salary schedule.

Professional partnerships. In addition to taking advantage (for oneself or one's students) of the offerings of a college or university, teachers may choose to become engaged in a genuine professional partnership with the professors. For some teachers, this may feel unfamiliar and initially a little uncomfortable. Many teachers have had little interaction with the academic world since they completed their own professional training, which may have been many years ago. In fact, for some teachers, the whole university milieu might remind them of a checkered academic background, where they remember just getting by. For them, the idea of voluntarily collaborating with academia might seem far-fetched.

Such attitudes, while understandable, may stand in the way of rich interaction. Practitioners and theoreticians need one another in their joint endeavor of advancing professional understanding of effective practice. Academics pursue their work in an environment that appears to many teachers to be isolated and rarefied. Practitioners, on the other hand, are engaged in the daily rough-and-tumble of working with young people. Neither group has all the answers, but each can make a contribution to professional understanding. Professors are able to stay current with the latest research findings from the academic community, while teachers are keenly aware of what is effective with their students. The work they can do together is superior to what either group can do individually.

It is important that in partnerships with university personnel the practicing educators not be made to feel that they are, in some way, less important to the effort than are the academics. Some professors convey the impression (perhaps unintentionally) that their role with local teachers is one of dispensing wisdom; as a result, the teachers tend to feel like second-class citizens in the partnership. However, thoughtful academics understand that the contributions of the two groups—academics and teachers—are equally important: University researchers may propose approaches the teachers would not have considered on their own, while the teachers work as a critical reality check on the academics.

Businesses

Businesses both large and small are integral to the communities in which they are located. Their employees are typically residents of the community, and the children of their employees attend local schools. Indeed, an important criterion when a large firm is deciding where to locate a new plant is the quality of the workforce as produced by the public schools. Furthermore, businesses look to the schools as the source of their future employees; it is important to them that the school system be of high caliber. For these reasons, in addition to a sense of community responsibility, many businesses seek ways to contribute to local education. Partnerships between businesses and schools can take several forms, as described below.

Program resources. Many businesspeople generously support the educational program in the schools. They may have surplus computer equipment, for example, of which the school district can make good use. In addition, they sometimes have well-equipped training rooms for their own use; when these are not booked for an in-house training, they make them available to the local schools for workshops.

In addition, some businesses support the local schools through the donation of time. Many companies permit their employees to tutor or read to students during lunch hours. Alternatively, some businesses allow their employees a full day a year to donate to any community agency; if the schools are set up to make use of this resource, it can constitute a real contribution. Furthermore, some businesses encourage their employees to serve as mentors to students; these relationships can have a powerful influence on students by supplementing the support they receive from their own families.

Opportunities for teachers. In some communities, businesses offer short-term summer employment to teachers. There are many advantages to these arrangements, and they go both directions. If a science teacher has a job assisting with research in a pharmaceutical company, for example, that teacher can see up close how lab work is conducted in the commercial sector. He may acquire up-to-date experience with the real world of scientific inquiry. At the same time, through these contacts, and principally through informal interactions, employees of the company come to know the teachers and learn about some of the challenges they face in their daily life with students. They can't help but have greater respect for the teachers than before the contact.

Internships for students. Some businesses are willing to allow students to work either after school during the year or during the summer. These opportunities are invaluable for students in that they enable them to see the real life of work and to put their studies in the context of authentic demands of the workplace.

Some businesspeople may need to be convinced of the value of student interns. They are naturally concerned with efficiency and may regard a student intern as a person who will require significant investment of time by an employee before she can be of any value. They may not recognize right away that simply the opportunity to shadow an individual or sit in on planning meetings provides invaluable insight into the workings of the business. Then, as time goes on, it will become clear which tasks the student might actually be able to assist with. Furthermore, a student's naïve-sounding suggestion might make a genuine contribution, partly due to the student's objectivity and detachment.

Teacher leaders play an important role in the business community. While principals are the official voice of the school and many have extensive networks, it is the teachers who frequently do the heavy lifting when it comes to things like making a presentation about a new program. It may be the teacher who developed the idea or at least has extensive knowledge of it. So while the principal's role is critical in developing partnerships with the business community, so is that of teacher leaders.

Public and Private Agencies

Most communities have public and private agencies, all offering opportunities for meaningful collaboration with the schools. In addition, they provide opportunities for teachers to offer service to the community. By contributing to community agencies, not only do teachers experience the satisfaction that can come only from giving service, but by their efforts they are also highly visible in the community.

Opportunities for staff community service are similar to, and in fact may be identical to, those for students. They can include volunteering in agencies that provide services in the community, reading to children at the library on Saturdays, or working in the corps of volunteers at the local hospital. These organizations depend on volunteers, and teachers are an important part of the community who can be tapped for service. The agencies and organizations fall into several different categories.

Public service agencies. Every community has its fire and police department, as well as water and environmental agencies and other governmental bodies. Although primarily concerned with public safety and governance, some of these agencies also have an educational mission and seek opportunities to work with schools. Most elementary schools schedule trips to the fire house or the town council meeting so that students are introduced to how they contribute to the life of the community. In addition, some teachers contribute time and energy to these community organizations by serving on a volunteer rescue squad or participating in projects to monitor water quality.

Social service agencies. In most communities, also, there are social service agencies, funded from either public or private sources. These may include a public health clinic, the animal welfare league, an environmental group, or a mental health agency. These agencies exist to serve the public; in their engagement with families in the community, educators are often aware of needs among their students and can refer them to the appropriate agency. And in making the referral, they must be able to convey an appropriate amount of information about the situation without violating norms of confidentiality.

But partnerships with social service agencies go far beyond referrals. Many boys and girls clubs, for example, have a well-developed after-school program for students. That program could be strengthened if one of its components was assistance for students with their homework; for this to be effective, someone in the school must ensure that agency personnel have access to the materials the students are learning. This is an ongoing task, requiring regular and frequent communication and planning sessions to ensure updated information.

Educational and cultural organizations. Most communities, in addition to the agencies providing social services, also have a number of educational and cultural groups, such as a historical museum, a public library, a zoo, a symphony orchestra, or a repertory company. Since these organizations are committed to supporting the education of citizens in a community, they may be seeking opportunities to work with the schools. Most orchestras offer special concerts for young people; many libraries provide space, and even assistance, for students to work on their homework and offer family reading hours for young children. In addition, these groups can play an active role in supporting student learning in the school. For example, if the staffs of the local historical and science museums are informed as to projects the students are working on, they will be able to offer substantive assistance when students come there after school. And they typically welcome classes for field trips, with staff dedicated to those programs. Margaret's BIG History Lesson from Chapter 1 illustrates where such efforts can lead.

Teachers can also make substantive contributions to educational and cultural institutions through their own service projects. They might serve as a docent in a museum or as an usher at the symphony or repertory theatre. Again, by engaging in service activities, teachers derive the satisfaction that accompanies such efforts and are visible in the community.

◇◇◇◇◇◇◇◇◇◇◇◇◇◇◇

If collaborations with community agencies are to be effective, of course, someone must take a leadership role in forging and maintaining them. This typically falls to teacher leaders who take the initiative in either creating these partnerships or maintaining and extending them. Figure 7.3 identifies ways teacher leaders might work with organizations outside the school district.

FIGURE 7.3
Partnerships with Universities, Businesses, and Community Agencies: Examples of Practice

Emerging teacher leaders work within their own classes to collaborate with outside groups. For example, they might

- Participate in a summer internship with a local business.
- Participate in a study with a university professor.
- Encourage their students to take advantage of a summer internship with a local business.
- Inform students (or parents) of after-school activities available through community agencies.

Setting	Established Teacher Leaders
Within Department or Team	Teacher leaders initiate partnerships between outside agencies and colleagues within their own departments or teams. For example, they might • Initiate an action research study with others in the team or department and professors from a local university. • Organize a tutoring program for students in the team with a local business. • Organize an effort by teachers in the department to make a presentation to the town council on an issue of student welfare.
Across the School	Teacher leaders establish partnerships with outside agencies affecting colleagues across the school. For example, they might • Make a presentation on behalf of the school to a business roundtable. • Coordinate the internships with local businesses. • Identify community resources that can provide speakers on different topics, and share this information with the entire faculty. • Organize a program for people in local businesses to serve as mentors to students.
Beyond the School	Teacher leaders participate in district, state, or national networks for enhancing partnerships between schools and external agencies. For example, they might • Serve on the statewide business/education roundtable. • Coordinate partnerships between the school district and, for instance, the library. • Teach a course in a local college or through the local library. • Develop a curriculum that takes advantage of the resources of a local nature center and disseminate it to teachers across the district. • Serve on a district committee to solicit agencies for community service needs. • Participate on a community committee to evaluate the adequacy of social services. • Offer a course in a prison or on a military installation.

Promoting and Developing Teacher Leadership

As educators become more and more convinced of the benefits to be derived from a school in which teacher leaders thrive, it is important to understand how schools can encourage their development. What are the school conditions that promote the emergence of teacher leaders, and what are the specific skills they need in order to do their work? Answering those questions is the purpose of Part III.

8

Promoting Teacher Leadership

Teacher leaders, as described in this book, can make a substantial contribution to a school's mission of educating all students. But, in order to make that contribution, teacher leaders must emerge. There are several issues involved in promoting and sustaining teacher leaders in schools. That is, if educators find the description of teacher leadership in Chapter 2 persuasive and they want teachers to develop and exhibit the skills described in Chapter 3, in a positive culture outlined in Chapter 4, in the areas of school life described in chapters 5 through 7, it is essential that both the conditions and capacity of the school support these teachers. There are many factors involved, including the actual skills of teachers. This chapter describes the issues integral to the challenge of promoting teacher leadership in your school.

◇◇◇◇◇◇◇◇◇◇◇◇◇◇◇◇◇◇

Supporting Conditions

It is not accidental that some schools and school districts promote teacher leaders and others do not—there are important conditions that must be in place if teacher leaders are to flourish. Some of these are cultural; others are structural. These two types of factors are considered separately in this section.

Cultural Factors

As described in Chapter 4, a school's culture is an essential enabling factor for a successful instructional program. That is, the school must embrace an optimistic and rigorous educational mission, and it must do so in an environment of respect and a culture of hard work and success. Moreover, and most important for this discussion, there must be a culture of professional inquiry in which teachers' examination of practice is an ongoing part of their work. Such examination is not a sign of weakness or inadequacy; rather, it should be undertaken by teachers as a routine part of their professional practice.

The culture to promote teacher leadership must be established and maintained first of all by district and site administrators. They set the tone for the building; they create the expectations for teachers and foster teachers' expectations for one another. This tone, although intangible, is real, and it can take time to develop if it has not been present previously. Although it is possible to analyze such a tone and extract its component parts, the general characteristics are easily recognized: an underlying sense of professionalism, an absence of "us versus them" thinking, and an acceptance of the deprivatization of practice. Administrators, while serving as formal heads of schools and ultimately being accountable for results, consider themselves part of a team and create that sense of team through their daily interactions with both teachers and support staff. Of course, if a teacher's performance has slipped, it is the administrator's responsibility to take action. But in other situations (and they are the vast majority), the atmosphere between principal and teachers is a collegial one.

Enlightened administrators recognize that achieving their aims of high-level student learning can happen only through the active engagement of teacher leaders. Thus, even if they were not committed to teacher leadership, self-interest would suggest that cultivation of teacher leaders is a wise move. The overwhelming size of the job of site administrator has been described in Chapter 2. Our focus here is on the aspects of a school's culture that will promote the emergence of teacher leaders.

A culture of risk taking. Improvement does not happen without new approaches being tried, and approaches that are new are unlikely to be completely successful the first time they are attempted. Administrators must convey the sense to all staff that the environment is a safe one in which to take professional risks. This suggests that there are no penalties for mistakes, and indeed, that lack of complete success is valued since it provides insights into what is not yet working as it should. This way of thinking supports the concept of high-quality mistakes, defined as those which provide valuable information when analyzed. Above all, no one is punished.

Democratic norms. In some schools there is an assumption that it is the administrators who make the decisions or who receive orders from downtown and then pass them along. Teacher are expected to comply with little question. For example, one teacher reported that "our principal listens to suggestions but has the final word. He works a step ahead, not side by side" (Hipp, 2003, p. 127). In contrast, an essential aspect of a culture supportive of teacher leadership is a prevailing norm of democracy. There are no favorites; all teachers can count on the ear of the principal and are confident that all ideas will be received warmly and evaluated on their merits. Furthermore, the norms of democracy extend to the status of teachers vis à vis administrators; administrators don't assume that just because they are the nominal leaders of the schools their ideas are necessarily better than the teachers in their buildings. In general, this suggests that the structure of the school, either formally or informally, is not overly hierarchical.

Teachers as professionals. If teachers are to emerge as leaders, they must be treated in such a manner that they are, and feel themselves to be, valued as professionals. This suggests that they are treated as people who not only follow the directives of supervisors but also make professional decisions on their own authority. Their opinions and judgments are valued, and they are part of a collegial community. There are times, to be sure, when the mandates from the state capitol or the central office must prevail, but even then it is in a context of professionalism.

As noted in Chapter 2, there are important historical reasons why teaching is not considered among the ranks of the "true" professions, such as architecture, medicine, or accounting. These reasons relate to the state's essential interest in the quality of schools for an educated citizenry and the virtual monopoly of public schools (resulting in a high degree of government oversight); the necessity for many school boards to hire teachers with emergency credentials (resulting in many inexperienced and in some cases underprepared teachers teaching children of poverty at a disproportionate rate); and the tradition of considering teaching to be women's work, a suitable career for women to take on around the edges of their perceived primary responsibility of raising a family. Teachers as professionals cannot thrive in such a culture, nor can teacher leaders as leaders of professionals. In schools that support the emergence of teacher leaders, the importance, complexity, and rigor of teaching are all recognized; teachers are treated with the respect accorded other professionals and are expected to behave in a way consistent with that standing.

Structural Factors

In addition to cultural factors that promote the development of teacher leadership, there are structural factors. That is, it matters how the school is organized, what opportunities are available, and how teachers can become engaged in shaping the work of the school. Some examples are provided below.

Mechanisms for involvement in school governance. Many schools are organized as instructional teams, houses, or departments. In those schools, there is typically a leadership team, comprising a member from each team within the school. In some cases, these are filled by those in designated roles, such as department chairs at a high school. In other cases, the membership of the leadership team is open to anyone expressing an interest, with the only stipulation being the necessity of ensuring balance among different teams or departments in the school. Teacher leaders tend to step into those roles—they volunteer to serve. But even when the roles are formally designated, teacher leaders understand how the structure works and use the leadership team as a sounding board for their ideas. However, none of this can occur if there is no governance structure in which teachers can become involved.

Mechanisms for proposing ideas. In some schools and school districts, there are formal opportunities for teachers to put forth ideas for consideration. In well-developed systems, these may take the form of minigrants for which teachers can apply to try a new approach or to learn something new and bring it back to the school for consideration. In applying for such minigrants, teachers are obliged to carefully think through what they intend to do and how they plan to go about it. Typically, the money involved is small (usually no more than $1,000 per grant), but it serves as a catalyst for teachers to think thoroughly about an idea and its possible benefits to the school. This mechanism can also be more informal, consisting of simply a recognized expectation that teachers will come forward with ideas.

Time for collaboration. Most of the work involved in teacher leadership requires time; it is typically undertaken in addition to a teacher's primary responsibility of teaching students. And if a project requires teachers to meet (as many do), that time must be available. In some schools, the master schedule permits opportunities for teams of teachers to engage in joint planning. But that is not always the case. In situations where the time is not built into the schedule, it must be carved from otherwise scheduled activities, or else be done either before or after school. Of course, if teachers are willing to be away from their classes and if there are funds to support them, substitutes can relieve teachers so they can meet with or observe their colleagues. Otherwise, teachers may find themselves obliged to engage in leadership activities outside the normal contract day.

Opportunities for skills acquisition. Very few teacher preparation programs include the skills necessary to serve as a teacher leader. This is understandable; the work of teaching is so complex and includes many different components that there is little time for the more advanced skills of leadership. As a result, most teachers, if they are to acquire the skills required to work as a leader with their colleagues, must develop them after they begin their practice. The skills themselves are described more fully in Chapter 9. In a school system committed to promoting the development of teacher leaders, opportunities to learn the skills needed for exercising such leadership are available to teachers as one of their options for professional development.

Inhibiting Conditions

Several factors can inhibit the development of teacher leadership. Again, there are both cultural and structural factors.

Cultural Factors

Culturally, inhibiting factors are primarily related to traditional norms of privacy and the solidarity of teachers in a hierarchical structure.

Administrators threatened by teacher leadership. Teacher leaders cannot emerge if principals and assistant principals jealously guard their turf and insist on maintaining rigid control. The hallmark of teacher leadership, after all, is taking initiative; teachers will seldom act on an idea if they sense that they will be beaten down at the outset by a principal who can't tolerate an invasion of her perceived area of sole responsibility. Teacher leadership cannot thrive in an atmosphere of fear. As noted earlier, administrators' reluctance to, as they see it, cede control over key functions of their role is self-defeating in the end. The vast and complex responsibilities of site administrators have evolved in such a manner as to extend beyond the expertise and energy of all but a very few extraordinary individuals. Administrators need the active engagement of teachers on their staffs in making substantive contributions to the school beyond teaching students. Furthermore, in one of the enduring paradoxes of leadership, when principals widen the conversation and permit teachers to take initiative in important matters of practice, their own authority is enhanced.

Some administrators may fear that when teacher leaders take initiative with a new project or approach, they will stir up a hornet's nest. That is, if there are underlying and unresolved tensions in the school, principals may fear that opening the door to greater teacher expression and leadership may release negative energy that they would prefer to keep under control. This could be seen as a real obstacle to teacher leadership, but the true obstacle lies in the underlying tensions; indeed, greater teacher expression and initiative might prove to be the first step in resolving them.

Teacher reluctance. Many teachers are reluctant to step up to propose a new program or idea; they feel they are stepping over the line of acceptable behavior. Alternatively, some teachers simply don't see themselves as leaders and would never describe themselves using that word. One teacher even said that if the term were used, she would run the other way! "I see myself as a 3rd grade teacher, not a teacher leader," she said. In other schools, teachers don't want to be seen by their colleagues as putting on airs. In fact, some teachers who achieve certification by the National Board for Professional Teaching Standards don't even announce it in their school for fear of being looked on askance by their colleagues. The Australians have a vivid term for this phenomenon: The "tall poppy syndrome," in which poppies that grow too tall get cut off so they are the same height as the others.

One source of teacher reluctance is captured in the phrase, "I just want to teach." Indeed, teaching well and engaging in ongoing professional improvement can be a lifelong endeavor. Teachers who elect not to become teacher leaders in the sense described in this book are no less professional than those who do; they are just putting their energies into refining their craft within their own classrooms rather than extending beyond it. But this does lead to the question of whether teachers should be spending their time on projects requiring leadership when they could be improving their teaching. This question has no definitive answer, although the ability to teach to at least a certain standard of excellence is an essential characteristic of a teacher who is considering taking on leadership activities. However, the projects undertaken by teacher leaders typically serve to improve the teaching of the teacher leaders themselves while enabling them to extend their influence in the school. That is, by taking initiative in their schools, teacher leaders generally reflect on their own practice, resulting in improved teaching. Indeed, it is precisely their expertise that gives credibility to the efforts of teacher leaders with other teachers.

Another source of teacher reluctance to assume leadership activities results from lack of confidence. A teacher might believe that he simply does not have professional insight or expertise that could be of value to others. In addition, some teachers might believe that even if they were to suggest a project, others would not be interested in becoming involved. This may be simply a matter of confidence; alternatively, it could be a matter of skill. Unless teachers have somehow acquired the complex planning and facilitation skills involved in leading others, they may not know how to go about it. Administrative support can resolve both of these issues; the matter of leadership skills is addressed in Chapter 9.

Structural Factors

Most schools are not organized to promote the development of teacher leadership: the school day, the school week, and the school year are all organized around a view of teaching that regards contact time with students as the entirety of the job. Any time teachers spend on professional learning or problem solving with their colleagues is regarded in some settings as extra and dispensable. Therefore, time for teachers to work on the craft of teaching and on improving the curriculum and how it is implemented with students must be carved out of time left over in the day. But it is much more than simply an issue of time: It is a matter of commitment. If professional work is regarded as important and teachers are regarded as professionals with important expertise, then the time will be built into the day and the calendar by those making the master schedule.

◇◇◇◇◇◇◇◇◇◇◇◇◇◇◇◇

Not all schools provide fertile ground for the emergence of teacher leaders. The factors related to teacher leadership are both cultural and structural and involve both teachers and administrators. If educators want to promote the development of teacher leaders, they must do it deliberately. And they must ensure that the conditions in place in the school support it.

Those educators wanting to cultivate an environment in which teacher leaders can thrive may want to conduct an audit of their school to ascertain the extent to which the conditions are right, and if the conditions are not supportive, to identify which areas need attention. The Appendix contains a sample teacher survey that could be used, as it is or modified, for this purpose. In addition, as indicated in the Appendix, it is important to analyze the structural aspects of the school's schedule and system for governance against the recommendations in this chapter regarding the conditions conducive to or inhibitive of the emergence of teacher leaders. Guidance for this analysis is also provided in the Appendix.

9

The Skills of Teacher Leadership

In preparation programs, teachers learn the skills of teaching. Few have the opportunity to acquire the skills needed to exercise leadership in their schools. If teachers are to be leaders, they must have the skills to do so. But what are those skills? The most important teacher leadership skills are described below.

Collaboration Skills

Because exercising leadership generally involves working with one's colleagues to investigate a situation and propose a plan to address it, the skills of collaboration are central to a teacher's success as a teacher leader. Some people may need to be convinced that these are skills worth cultivating. After all, what can be so difficult about running a meeting? We do it every day with our students! However, working with colleagues is different from teaching students; adults are, in some ways, more demanding. What follows is a brief overview of the skills needed for successful collaboration with colleagues.

Establishing Group Norms

It is essential for members of any group to know that they are safe, that their ideas will not be ridiculed or dismissed out of hand. Therefore, before a group of teachers begins its real work, it is important to hammer out both the expectations of the group as a whole and what members of the group can expect from one another. These items will range from the mundane (committing to coming to meetings, coming on time) to items that structure the conversation (refraining from interrupting one another, maintaining an open mind, participating actively, not criticizing an idea prematurely). Group norms or ground rules might have been established by an entire school staff to be used in large faculty meetings; in that case, they can simply be applied to smaller teacher collaborative work.

Selecting a Leader

In some situations, it is obvious that the leader is the individual who has convened the group. In that case, that individual would be expected to serve as leader or facilitator of the group's meetings. In other situations it is not necessarily evident who the leader should be. It is important to have an individual at each meeting serve as facilitator, but it does not have to be the same person at each meeting. In fact, if that role rotates, everyone on the team gains insight into the demands of the facilitator role.

Determining Roles

It may be advantageous to assign members of the group to certain roles: note taker, flip chart writer, and time keeper. Such roles may be too formal for some groups, but in some situations, it is a good idea to have those roles filled.

Facilitation Skills

Arguably, the most critical skill for a teacher leader is the ability to facilitate dialogue among teachers. After all, the purpose of teacher leadership is to mobilize others around a common purpose; it is through the process of discussion that a group develops common understanding and builds the intellectual capital of the school. There are many facilitation skills, and entire books are written on the subject. What follows here is a brief summary. Many of these tasks may be performed by any member of the group, but at the very least, the leader should be able to do these things.

Introducing a Topic

A group leader poses a question or introduces a topic in some way. Ideally, the topic is presented in an invitational manner, one that draws others into the discussion. There are many ways to introduce a topic, and the specific details will depend, of course, on what people know before they agree to join the work. A sample topic introduction is, "I've been noticing that _____, and I wonder whether any of you have seen the same thing?"

Presenting a New Idea

Someone may have a unique way to look at a situation; these outside-of-the-box ideas should be encouraged. And if norms have been established, someone offering an off-the-wall idea will not fear ridicule. A member of the group might say, "I wonder whether it would help if we were to ____," or, "I heard recently about a new approach—it sounded good to me."

Leading the Discussion

In a productive group, members of the group have ideas to contribute to the conversation. This is where the leader's facilitation skills come into play and may occasionally be challenged. It is important that individuals are not permitted to dominate, that all views receive a thorough and respectful hearing, and that members of the group listen actively to one another. In ensuring the participation of everyone, it may be necessary to say to an individual, "What do you think about this, Joe? Have any of your students responded in this manner?" or, "Perhaps we could allow others to share their views."

At times, it may also be necessary to remind the group of process matters, such as the rules for brainstorming if that is an approach to be used. In addition, there are differences between dialogue, advocacy, and inquiry in the manner in which topics are discussed. These group process tools are described in, among other sources, *The Handbook for SMART School Teams* (Conzemius & O'Neill, 2002).

Keeping the Group on Track

It is a fact of group work that some individuals have a tendency to stray from the topic or to use any discussion as a forum in which to advocate for a pet idea. Redirecting the contributions of these people without making them feel shut down can be difficult. It is, however, essential if the group's work is to proceed. Endless bird walks (or rambles) are discouraging to those in the group who are task oriented, and they can slow down the work of the group. A possible intervention in such situations is, "I would like to remind all of us of the issue we are exploring."

Clarifying

There are times when a group member does not state a position clearly, and others in the group, as a result of not understanding what was said, may respond to a different point altogether. An important skill of facilitation, then, is being alert to when there is confusion as to meaning and when a point requires clarification. In this situation, a group member or the leader might say something like, "I wonder whether you mean _____, or is it more like _____?" Or in a discussion about grading, a leader might say, "Charles, it sounds as though you are afraid that if we are too lenient about how we grade homework, students just won't do it, whereas you, Alison, appear to think that by grading homework harshly, we are not sufficiently sensitive to those students who simply can't get it done at home. Would that be an accurate summary of your thoughts?"

Mediating

Not every member of a work group sees a situation in exactly the same way; indeed, that is the value of enlisting the participation of a number of people with different perspectives. It is in the dialogue, in hearing various points of view and being reminded of factors that individuals may have overlooked, that the work can move forward. But because individuals see things differently, there may be strongly held positions that are difficult to reconcile. In mediating discussions, then, it is important to try to isolate the sources of the difference and to look "behind" the differences for explanations of them. For example, following the previous example about grading, the facilitator might ask, "Is there an approach to grading that could accommodate the perspectives of both Charles and Alison?" or, "What John and Ruth have been saying sound to me like different aspects of the same thing, and that is _____. What do others think?"

Summarizing and Integrating

At some point in the discussion, it may be important to take a step back and summarize what has been said to that point. Discussions can ramble, and every now and then it is important to take stock, especially prior to the conclusion of a session. It is at this point that the flip chart scribe or note taker can summarize where the group is in its deliberations, what the group thinks should be done next, and who has offered to do what. The summarizing and integrating can happen at any point during a discussion; following a conversation in which many different points of view have been presented, an individual might say something like, "We have agreed that we should analyze the enrollment patterns of girls and boys in advanced courses. Who would be willing to do this prior to our next meeting?"

Dealing with Negativity

There are individuals who take the position that any course of action proposed has been tried already, to no avail: "We tried that once, and it didn't work!" Typically, these people do not elect to join a study group to explore an issue but let others try to find effective new approaches, assuming that new approaches will not succeed. However, there are situations when an individual in a work group takes a negative attitude toward the project, throwing cold water on suggestions made by others. This is when the group's norms come into play; the leader may have to remind the person (gently and in private) that one of the agreements made by the group at the outset was that they would respect everyone's views and give them a fair hearing. If there are good reasons why an approach is not likely to succeed, those reasons should be fully aired. But negativity for its own sake is contrary to the group's expectations and counterproductive to achieving its goals.

Knowing When to Summon Outside Expertise

Teachers may want to explore some issues that require additional knowledge. A well-informed expert can save a group hours of time and can point them in a productive direction. For example, if a study group is considering the issue of grading and how to make the grading system yield maximum student commitment to work, members might invite a psychologist who specializes in human motivation to summarize current research. Then, in their deliberations, group members can make use of the insights from this expert in framing their own approach.

Planning Skills

When teacher leaders embark on a project, when they decide that an issue warrants an exploration, and when they enlist the participation of colleagues, they must engage in planning. It is not sufficient to sit around and discuss something or to wring one's hands. What is needed fairly early in the process is an approach to action, and that requires planning.

Much has been written about planning, and most of the literature takes a top-down approach: have a goal, collect baseline data, consider alternative approaches, select the best approach, implement the plan, collect data, and evaluate the action. For a well-defined problem with a known set of alternative solutions, such an approach is both efficient and effective. However, many issues in which teacher leaders are likely to be involved are much messier than that approach would suggest. Educators see a situation and can identify a problem or a pattern that appears to represent a problem or recognize an opportunity to implement a better approach for their students. Acting on these situations requires planning skills, but not necessarily the top-down ones represented by much of the planning literature.

So what are the planning skills needed by teacher leaders? They are not completely different from those recommended in a more traditional, top-down approach, but they are less formal.

Problem Posing or Problem Finding

Not all situations are well defined. Not all problems are even easily recognizable as problems. For example, Margaret, the teacher who created the BIG History Lesson in Chapter 1, was not faced with a traditional problem. Instead, she saw a situation (field trips with her students) that she realized could be improved. That recognition—the lack of engagement shown by her students with the content of the museum—could be labeled a problem. She recognized an opportunity to explore options in search of a better approach. Similarly, Elena's interest in looping did not arise from a problem for which the revised approach to teacher assignment would be a solution. Instead, she was persuaded by professional reading and conversation that this was an approach that might prove effective in her school. On the other hand, Tom, in his concern for the underperformance of girls and members of minority groups, saw a more traditional problem. What he actually observed was not the problem itself but a symptom of a deeper problem. It is that deeper problem that he sought, with his colleagues, to better understand. Both Margaret and Tom had to engage in sophisticated analysis of the situation in order to begin framing a new approach. In so doing, they could have chosen from many recognized methods of analysis.

In complex systems, this is not unusual. Look at an example from urban planning: many citizens consider the traffic around their cities a major problem. This situation frequently leads city councils to build more roads to relieve the pressure on existing roads. But in fact, the traffic may be merely a reflection or symptom of something else, namely diffused housing and employment patterns and lack of public transportation.

These, taken together, require most residents to drive a car to work. Hence, a solution to the problem—building more roads—might actually, by encouraging more development, make the problem of excessive traffic worse.

In schools, when confronted with a problem, the first requirement for educators is to understand it. They must determine whether what they have observed is actually a problem or a symptom of something more complex. For example, high school teachers might be concerned that many students don't do their homework and don't seem concerned about it. Why might this be the case? In trying to understand it, the teachers will typically proceed through most, if not all, of these steps:

Brainstorming. What might be causing the observed situation? There are any number of possible factors that should all be considered. For example, it is first important to know whether there are patterns in the noncompletion of homework. Is it all students or only some students? Is it possible that teachers don't have consistent expectations? Or that teachers have not communicated their expectations clearly? Or that the student culture requires students, in order to be cool, to not take schoolwork seriously? Or that some students' home lives make it difficult for them to complete their homework? Or that they don't understand the assignments? Or that there are no consequences for either doing or not doing homework? Or that students don't understand the purposes of homework? Any of these explanations (or others) is possible, and indeed, several may be operating simultaneously.

Determining what would count as evidence. To investigate possible explanations for the observed phenomenon, it is essential to narrow down the possibilities using solid information. For the questions about noncompletion of homework, the educators involved need to decide what information they would need to ascertain the cause. This is not an insignificant matter, since data collection of any type is time consuming.

In general, there are two fundamental types of data: perceptual data and hard data. Hard data, as the term suggests, can be summarized in numbers, such as participation rates in advanced courses (from Tom's example) or observations of how many students were paying attention to the museum docents (in Margaret's example). Hard data are factual and difficult to refute. Perceptual data, on the other hand, reflect people's perceptions: what they believe, or how they report themselves to be treated by others. Perceptions are the important factor in many situations, and it is critical to know what those are. For example, Margaret's students might report that they feel bored at the museum; minority students in Tom's school might report that they don't feel welcome in the advanced classes. In the homework example, some of the questions—whether the noncompletion of homework is uniform across the school or particularly pronounced in certain courses or among certain students, for example—are empirical questions that can be answered with hard data. Students not being clear about expectations, on the other hand, or students lacking (or believing they are lacking) the knowledge and skill to complete assignments is a perceptual matter that can be verified only by eliciting perceptual data.

Collecting hard data is straightforward enough, although it may be tedious. Records may need to be analyzed or homework completion rates collected and compared for different groups of students. For perceptual information, there are several principal methodologies:

• *Interviews.* The preferred method to learn detailed information from individuals is the interview, in which questions are typically determined in advance but the conversation is allowed to go in any direction that emerges during the interview itself. The disadvantage of interviews is the time required to complete them. In addition, there is danger in interviews that the atmosphere will not be sufficiently safe; interviewees may fear that they cannot give their honest opinion.

• *Focus groups.* A focus group permits in-depth and semistructured exploration of an issue, but with a group of people rather than individuals. In a focus group, a small number of individuals (usually no more than 15) is assembled to explore a specific topic or issue. The convener of the group typically has a few prepared questions but permits the conversation to extend beyond the exact questions if such an extension is productive. This is a useful strategy when one is not sure of all the issues or when it is possible that the composition of the group will spark different ways of looking at a situation because of differing perspectives. The results of focus group discussions are useful in framing questions for a survey. In focus groups, however, as in interviews, individuals may not feel adequately safe to be completely honest.

• *Surveys.* Surveys are constructed to obtain the views of a large number of people in an efficient manner. Questions are framed so that respondents can indicate their views, usually on some sort of sliding scale. The questions must be clear and suitable to the individuals to whom they are directed. Children as young as 9 years old may be surveyed, but the questions must be appropriate. It is also important to determine whether everyone in a certain population must be surveyed or whether a sample would be sufficient. If a sample is used, it must of course be representative of the total population.

Another advantage of a survey is that individuals can respond anonymously. In a culture where people fear retribution, this is not an insignificant factor.

An example of ways to identify evidence that would help teachers solve the homework noncompletion problem is shown in Figure 9.1.

FIGURE 9.1
Identification of Evidence

Which students do not regularly complete their homework? Why?

Subquestions	Possible Evidence	Comments
Is it all students who don't complete homework? Only students in advanced classes? Only students in low-level classes? Only high-performing or low-performing students? Only students of certain ethnicities or income levels?	Teachers' homework records	Teachers should do this analysis of their own records, since only they are familiar with their students. But the categories to be analyzed should be decided in advance: gender, ethnicity, level of class, etc.
Are teachers' expectations for homework consistent?	Teacher course outlines and expectations	This analysis is best done by teachers as a group and might yield a decision to bring outlines and expectations into alignment.
Do students understand their teachers' expectations about homework?	Student survey	It is important that student responses be anonymous. Teachers should determine whether each teacher's students should be tallied separately.
Does student culture "require" students to not take schoolwork seriously in order to be "cool"?	Student focus groups, student survey	The questions for focus groups should be framed carefully; the ensuing discussion will yield good material to use in designing a student survey.
Do the demands or home conditions of some students' family lives make it difficult for them to complete their homework?	Student focus groups, student survey, conversations with parents	The focus groups should include students who may have extensive home responsibilities or poor conditions in which to study; the discussion can help teachers design a larger survey. If it is possible to conduct conversations with parents, additional information might be obtained for a parent outreach program.

(Figure continued on next page)

FIGURE 9.1 Identification of Evidence *(continued)*		
Subquestions	**Possible Evidence**	**Comments**
Do students understand the assignments?	Student survey, conversations with (or survey of) parents	It is important that student responses be anonymous. Teachers should determine whether each teacher's students should be tallied separately. Parents, particularly those of young students, will have insights as to whether their children are able to complete their homework independently.
Do students see the value of homework assignments?	Student focus groups, student survey	If students regard homework assignments as "busy work," pointless, or unrelated to what they are learning, they are less likely to take them seriously. If, in addition, teachers impose harsh penalties for noncompletion, the entire situation may feel punitive to students. Focus groups and surveys, analyzed by different classes, will reveal student views.

Collecting and analyzing the relevant data. Once a committee has determined what would count as evidence for the question they are exploring, the data must actually be collected and analyzed. As important as this step is, it should not be allowed to become overwhelming. It is possible to become tangled up in the endless work of collecting information in what has been termed "analysis paralysis." The concept of elegance is useful here in assembling sufficient information from all necessary sources (either hard or perceptual data) to understand the question being explored. There are no hard rules about how much is enough, but it should be enough to know which of the various possibilities identified during the brainstorming were accurate. A plan is useful for this step; the organizer in Figure 9.2 can help the committee proceed with such a plan.

Action and Evaluation Skills

When a situation is finally understood, educators are in a position to formulate a plan of action. The components of the plan will be dictated by information obtained during the phases of brainstorming and data collection. That is, once the situation is understood, the action needed will be evident. But even when it is evident what the action should be, there must be a plan.

FIGURE 9.2 Plan for Gathering Information		
Directions: For the questions under consideration, determine what information should be collected to serve as evidence of the school's practices.		
Evidence (e.g., Focus Group, Student Survey, Conversations with Parents, Analysis of Documents)	**Individuals Responsible**	**Time Line**

Setting Goals

As part of planning action, educators must determine first of all what the goal of the action is. To continue with the homework example, the broad goal is for more students to complete homework assignments. Depending on information derived from the information collection and analysis, teachers may have learned that students are not clear about teachers' expectations regarding homework and that they don't see the value of the assignments. It is possible, of course, that the students are correct in their perceptions: the assignments may have little value. Therefore, the team working on this issue may set two goals: to establish clear expectations that are understood by students and to make homework assignments valuable to student learning, as well as to be seen by students to be valuable.

Determining Evidence of Success

How will the team know it has been successful? How will educators know that they have achieved their goals? The evidence of success is likely to be similar to the evidence that identified the need in the first place: in the homework example, students, when surveyed, would report that they understand the expectations for homework assignments and find them of value.

Planning Actions

Next, the team must decide who is responsible for each of the actions. They must make a time line and identify needed resources. When is it reasonable for actions to be done? By whom? And what resources (release time, materials) will be needed? Figure 9.3 can be helpful with this planning.

Maintaining Logs of Activities

Once educators have begun work on their plan, it is usually helpful to keep track of what they do. This is not intended to generate large amounts of paperwork; rather, the records should be organized such that they can be completed quickly, with a single line for each activity (see Figure 9.4). These logs provide a useful documentation of what actions the team took to address a situation; if a group subsequently addresses the same or a similar issue, these records could be very valuable.

◇◇◇◇◇◇◇◇◇◇◇◇◇◇◇◇◇

Some teacher leaders emerge spontaneously from the life of schools; they emerge without conscious or formal effort on the part of school or district administrators. By articulating the skills of teacher leadership and by deliberately incorporating these skills into professional development programs, a school or district will increase the chances that teacher leaders will be available to improve the school's program.

Of course, the skills of teacher leadership are beneficial for all teachers, not only their leaders, to acquire. When every member of a school faculty has been introduced to the fundamentals of group process and facilitation, of problem posing and problem solving, of data collection and analysis, then every project undertaken in the school, regardless of who is directing it, will proceed more smoothly. Furthermore, when all teachers have these skills, then any of them will be able to assume leadership roles when and if they choose to.

FIGURE 9.3

Action Plan

Teachers or Team: _____ School: _____

Grade(s): _____ Subject(s): _____ Date: _____

1. Based on your analysis, what, specifically, is your goal?

2. What would success regarding this goal look like? How will you know when you have achieved it? What would count as evidence of success?

3. Describe the activities you will do to work toward your goal, and their time lines:

    Activity   Time Line

4. What resources will you need to better achieve your goal?

FIGURE 9.4
Log of Activities

Teacher or Team: _____   School: _____

Grade(s): _____   Subject(s): _____   Date: _____

Goal: _____

Date	Activity	Comments

Appendix: School Audit

Not every school is equally likely to witness the emergence of teacher leaders. In some schools, the environment is highly conducive to leadership from teachers, while other schools retain a traditional bureaucratic structure. The culture required for meaningful school improvement has been described in Chapter 4, and the conditions supporting the development of teacher leadership have been outlined in Chapter 8. But describing those conditions leads to the next question: How can educators know the extent to which their school reflects that culture and those conditions?

An audit is a way of answering that question. It consists of the collection of information about structures and procedures, as well as surveys of both students and staff. The results of these instruments can be analyzed to determine the aspects of the school and its culture that serve to promote the development of teacher leaders and those aspects that could inhibit such development.

The sample instruments provided here are intended as tools for practitioners to begin their own investigation of the conditions in their schools. They could be used as they are, but educators may want to make adjustments so that they reflect their own situations. The student survey relates to the school's overall culture; the teacher survey encompasses both the general school culture and those aspects of the school that support or inhibit the development of teacher leaders.

Analysis of Structures

An important contributor to the emergence and work of teacher leaders lies in the structures in place in the school for collaborative work by teachers and the procedures for governance. Teacher *perceptions* regarding these matters are included in the teacher leadership survey; the purpose of the following six questions is to document the actual structural arrangements.

Availability of Time for Teachers to Work Together

1. To what extent does the master schedule enable teachers to work together? For example, do teachers have common planning time? Is there a regularly scheduled late arrival or early dismissal for students to permit extended work time?

2. How frequently are teachers able to observe one another's classes? Is this something that can be done regularly, or must teachers locate a replacement?

School Governance

3. What are the arrangements for decision making in the school? Is there a leadership council or similar body consisting of teachers from each department or team?

4. What role does the leadership council play in making decisions? Does it serve as a rubber stamp for decisions made elsewhere (by site or district office administrators) or are its deliberations an integral part of the decision-making process?

5. What mechanisms are in place for all teachers to contribute to the work of the leadership council? Do teachers make presentations to the council? Do they have the opportunity to comment on new policies and programs prior to implementation?

6. What sorts of decisions are made by the leadership council? Are they central to the instructional program and the school's operations (for example, the master schedule or assessment practices), or are they peripheral to the central work of the school?

School Culture

As noted in Chapter 4, the quality of initiatives undertaken by teacher leaders is closely related to aspects of general school culture. And while educators can (and should) work to deliberately improve their school's culture, the *perception* of that culture (by both students and teachers) is a critical aspect of the culture itself. The surveys on the following pages are designed to elicit the views of teachers and students regarding that culture.

Student Survey

Any student survey must be written in such a manner as to be appropriate to the age of the students. Furthermore, it is important that the questions be phrased so that they ask about the *school and teachers collectively,* not about individual teachers. Most of the questions are phrased such that "SA" represents the response most supportive of a positive school culture. However, the opposite is true about the response to question 3; educators should bear this in mind when tabulating the results.

Teacher Survey

A survey of teacher perception is the only way to tap some realities about the school's professional culture. As educators learn more about schools as institutions, they discover that cultural aspects of the school have an enormous impact on the school's effectiveness with its students.

The teacher survey offered here invites teachers to select, from several options, the statement that best describes the situation in their school with respect to several aspects of culture. By tabulating the results, educators can get a good sense of the tone of the school; the results might well point to areas that could be improved.

◇◇◇◇◇◇◇◇◇◇◇◇◇◇◇◇

The information that your school or district gathers from the three parts of the audit can be used to strengthen professional practice. The whole school community can benefit from the emergence and efforts of teacher leaders.

Student Survey			

Directions: For the following statements, think about your school overall and indicate whether you strongly disagree (SD), disagree (D), agree (A), or strongly agree (SA) with each statement.

In my school . . .	SD	D	A	SA
1. My teachers ask for my opinion.				
2. Other students respect me for who I am.				
3. Other students make fun of me or my ideas.				
4. My teachers believe that I am smart.				
5. I want to work for good grades.				
6. I know that if I work hard I can get good grades.				
7. The grades I receive are fair.				
8. School and classroom rules are reasonable.				
9. I have had a chance to help develop or revise the school's rules.				
10. I have had a chance to help develop our classroom rules.				
11. My teachers give me extra help when I need it.				
12. There are lots of activities around the school to be involved in.				
13. I am able to help other students, either younger students or those in my own class.				

	Teacher Survey

Directions: Indicate the statement that best reflects the situation in your school.

Professional culture

1. Expectations for professional learning

_____ If I don't want to work on improving my teaching, that's ok.

_____ My colleagues and I are encouraged to improve our practice; some do so.

_____ Most teachers in the school work on improving their practice.

_____ Improving one's practice is expected of all teachers and is central to the definition of being a teacher.

2. Deprivatization of practice

_____ It makes me nervous for other teachers to visit my class, and I never or rarely observe in theirs.

_____ Although it makes me nervous, I observe my colleagues every now and then, and I allow them to observe me.

_____ If they want to, teachers can observe in one another's classrooms; it happens fairly frequently among some teachers.

_____ Teachers are expected to observe one another's classrooms frequently, and administrators support us in making these visits.

3. A culture that supports risk taking

_____ I am afraid for my administrator to watch me trying anything new; it might go badly and be used against me.

_____ Administrators say that they want us to try new approaches, but I am not sure they mean it.

_____ My colleagues and I are encouraged to try new approaches, but the administrators keep a hands-off attitude.

_____ I am encouraged by administrators to try new things; either administrators or other teachers come to watch and we work together to improve.

4. Professionalism of teachers

_____ Administrators act as though they have all the answers to how I should teach; I am not asked for my professional opinion on best approaches.

_____ Administrators solicit the views of teachers, but then tell us what we should do in our work with students.

_____ My colleagues and I have considerable autonomy in what we do with our students, but the big issues are decided by the administrators.

_____ In deciding how to teach students, teachers and administrators work collegially; the administrators sometimes have good ideas, but they don't believe that just because they are administrators their ideas are better than those of the teachers.

(Survey continued on next page)

Teacher Survey *(continued)*

Professional culture

5. Teacher attitudes toward teacher initiative

_____ If I were to attain professional recognition (e.g., certification by the National Board for Professional Teaching Standards), I am not sure I would mention it at school.

_____ When I have an idea for something new, other teachers are quick to point out its disadvantages.

_____ My colleagues treat my ideas with respect and give them serious consideration.

_____ Lots of teachers have good ideas for improving our program; we work together to explore them more deeply.

6. Teacher attitude toward professional recognition

_____ If I were to attain professional recognition, I would tell a few close friends and colleagues at work.

_____ If I were to attain professional recognition, I would expect it to enhance my reputation at school.

_____ If I were to attain professional recognition, I predict that the school would throw a party in my honor.

School governance

7. Decision making

_____ All important structural decisions for the school (budgeting, master schedule, etc.) are made by administrators with no consultation with teachers.

_____ Administrators invite me and my colleagues to offer ideas about organizational matters; I don't know whether they actually pay attention to the ideas.

_____ There is a formal structure for making decisions, and the team leaders and department chairs meet regularly with administrators; however, I am informed of what they decide only after the fact.

_____ My colleagues and I have lots of opportunities to offer ideas for organizational decisions; these decisions reflect the contributions of teachers.

8. Opportunities to take initiative

_____ I never propose a new idea because I know it will just be shot down.

_____ Every now and then, my colleagues and I muster the courage to make a proposal to the administration; these have received some consideration.

_____ I feel that ideas I have would be welcomed by administrators.

_____ Teachers are actively encouraged to propose new ideas; sometimes there is even funding available to support their implementation.

(Survey continued on next page)

Teacher Survey *(continued)*

School governance
9. Time for collaboration

_____ If I want to work with other teachers on a new idea, we have to do it before or after school.

_____ Administrators say that they think we should work together on new ideas, but they have done nothing to make it possible.

_____ Administrators appreciate the value of time for us to work together, but they have not institutionalized it into the school's schedule and don't actively help us arrange it.

_____ When teachers need time to work together or to observe in one another's classrooms, the administrators help us find it, even covering our classes when needed. The schedule builds in time for collaboration.

References

Aronson, J. (2004, November). The threat of stereotype. *Educational Leadership, 62*(3), 14–19.

Barone, W. P. (2003). *Creating a culture of teacher leadership.* Unpublished paper.

Carnegie Forum on Education and the Economy. (1986). *A nation prepared: Teachers for the 21st century.* Report of the Task Force on Teaching as a Profession. Washington, DC: The Forum. (ERIC Document Reproduction Service no. ED 268 120).

Collinson, V. (2004). Teachers caught in acts of leading, learning, and teaching. *Teacher Education and Practice, 17*(4), 363–385.

Conzemius, A., & O'Neill, J. (2002). *The handbook for SMART school teams.* Bloomington, IN: National Educational Service.

Costa, A., & Garmston, R. (1994). *Cognitive Coaching: A foundation for renaissance schools.* Norwood, MA: Christopher-Gordon.

Costa, A., & Kallick, B. (2000). *Discovering and exploring habits of mind.* Alexandria, VA: Association for Supervision and Curriculum Development.

Council of Chief State School Officers. (1996). *Interstate school leaders licensure consortium: Standards for school leaders.* Washington, DC: Author.

Danielson, C. (1996). *Enhancing professional practice: A framework for teaching.* Alexandria, VA: Association for Supervision and Curriculum Development.

Danielson, C., & McGreal, T. (2000). *Teacher evaluation to enhance professional practice.* Alexandria, VA: Association for Supervision and Curriculum Development.

Darling-Hammond, L. (1996). What matters most: A competent teacher for every child. *Phi Delta Kappan, 78*(3), 193–200.

Deal, T. E., & Peterson, K. D. (1999). *Shaping school culture: The heart of leadership.* San Francisco, Jossey-Bass.

Dewey, J. (1903). Democracy in education. *Elementary School Teacher, 4*(4), 192-204.

Dweck, C. (1999). *Self theories: Their role in motivation, personality, and development.* Philadelphia: Psychology Press.

Dweck, C., & Sorich, L. A. (1999). Mastery oriented thinking. In C. R. Snyder (Ed.), *Coping: The psychology of what works.* New York: Oxford University.

Elmore, R. F. (2000). *Building a new structure for school leadership.* New York: The Albert Shanker Institute. Available: http://www.shankerinstitute.org/education.html.

Fantuzzo, J., McWayne, C., Perry, M. A., & Childs, S. (2004). Multiple dimensions of family involvement and their relations to behavioral and learning competencies for urban, low-income children. *School Psychology Review, 33*(4), 467–480. Available: www.nasponline.org/publications/spr334fantuzzo.pdf.

Fullan, M. (2001). *Leading in a culture of change.* San Francisco: Jossey-Bass.

Grossman, F. D., & Ancess, J. (2004, November). Narrowing the gap in affluent schools. *Educational Leadership, 62*(3), 70–73.

Hargreaves, A. (In press). Sustaining educational change. *Educational Administration Quarterly.*

Hipp, K. (2003). *Professional learning communities: Initiation to implementation.* Lanham, MD: Scarecrow Press.

Howard, P. K. (2004, December 3). You can't buy your way out of a bureaucracy [Editorial]. *New York Times,* p. A29.

Hunter, M. (1978). *Improved instruction.* El Segundo, CA: TIP Publications.

Hunter, M. (1982). *Mastery teaching.* Thousand Oaks, CA: Corwin.

Interstate New Teacher Assessment and Support Consortium (INTASC). (1992). *Model standards for beginning teacher licensing, assessment and development: A resource for state dialogue.* Washington, DC: Council of Chief State School Officers.

Jackson, D. B. (2003). Education reform as if student agency mattered: Academic microcultures and student identity. *Phi Delta Kappan, 84*(8), 579–585.

Katzenmeyer, M., & Moller, G. (2001). *Awakening the sleeping giant: Helping teachers develop as leaders.* Thousand Oaks, CA: Corwin.

Kolb, D. A. (1984). *Experimental learning: Experience as the source of learning and development.* Englewood Cliffs, NJ: Prentice-Hall.

Landsman, J. (2004, November). Confronting the racism of low expectations. *Educational Leadership, 62*(3), 28–32.

Lewin, L., & Shoemaker, B. J. (1998). *Great performances: Creating classroom-based assessment tasks.* Alexandria, VA: Association for Supervision and Curriculum Development.

Lewis, C. C. (2002). *Lesson study: A handbook of teacher-led instructional change.* Philadelphia: Research for Better Schools.

Lieberman, A., & Miller, L. (2004). *Teacher leadership.* San Francisco: Jossey-Bass.

Little, J. W. (1995). Contested ground: The basis of teacher leadership in high schools that restructure. *Elementary School Journal, 96*(1), 47–63.

Loucks-Horsley, S. (1996). Professional development for science education: A critical and immediate challenge. In R. Bybee (Ed.), *National standards and the science curriculum of the biological sciences curriculum study.* Dubuque, IA: Kendall/Hunt Publishing.

Marzano, R. J. (2000). *Transforming classroom grading.* Alexandria, VA: Association for Supervision and Curriculum Development.

McKibben, S. (2004, April). The power of student voice. *Educational Leadership, 61*(7), 79–81.

Mitchell, R. (1992). *Testing for learning: How new approaches to evaluation can improve American schools.* New York: The Free Press.

National Board for Professional Teaching Standards. (1989). *What teachers should know and be able to do.* Washington, DC: National Board for Professional Teaching Standards.

Sanders, J., & Cotton Nelson, S. (2004, November). Closing gender gaps in science. *Educational Leadership, 62*(3), 74–77.

Secretary's Commission on Achieving Necessary Skills (SCANS Report). (1991). Washington, DC: U.S. Department of Labor.

Simmons, J. (2004). *Transforming urban school districts: Strategy and practice for results.* Chicago: Strategic Learning Initiatives.

Spillane, J., Halverson, R., & Diamond, J. B. (2001, April). Investigating school leadership practice: A distributed perspective. *Educational Researcher, 30*(3), 23–28.

Steele, C. M., & Aronson, J. (1995). Stereotype threat and the intellectual test performance of African Americans. *Journal of Personality and Social Psychology, 69*(5), 797–811.

Stiggins, R. J. (1994). *Student-centered classroom assessment.* New York: Merrill.

Urbanski, A. (2004, November). *Union-district collaboration to build high-performing schools for all students.* Conference report presented at Quality Matters! Getting Our Best Teachers Where They are Needed Most: WestEd.

Waters, T., Marzano, R. J., & McNulty, B. (2003). *Balanced leadership: What 30 years of research tells us about the effect of leadership on student achievement.* Aurora, CO: Mid-continent Research for Education and Learning.

Wiggins, G. (1993). *Assessing student performance: Exploring the purpose and limits of testing.* San Francisco: Jossey-Bass.

Index

Page references for figures are indicated with an *f* after the page number.

achievement gap, closing the, 21
assessment
    formative, 96–97
    purpose of, 92–94
    school audit, 147–153, 151–153*f*
    summative, 94–95
    teaching standards, 97–100
attendance policies, 68–69

BIG lesson concept, 3–4
business-school partnerships, 118–119

change management, 18
classroom environment, 101
Cognitive Coaching technique, 102
collaboration
    ground rules for, 133–134
    Japanese lesson study, 102
    school audit, 148
    school structure supporting, 128–129
colleges
    school communication with, 114–115
    school partnerships with, 115, 117–118, 122*f*
collegiality. *See also* leadership skills
    in culture of professional inquiry, 54–57, 86
    de-privatization of practice and, 85–86
    leadership and, 38
    respectful interactions for, 48–49

commitment, leadership skill of, 36–37, 42
communication
    with families of students, 105–110, 111*f*
    with other district schools, 113–114
    with other educators, 110, 112, 116*f*
    with postsecondary institutions, 114–115
    within the school, 112
community education, 109
community partnerships, 115, 117–121, 122*f*
compensation issues, 23–24
confidence
    building in teachers, 42
    leadership and, 38–39
contested ground. *See* teacher leadership: obstacles
    to
contracts, 23–24
Costa, Art, 36
courage, leadership skill of, 38
creativity, leadership skill of, 39
culture in schools. *See* school culture
curriculum, attributes of well-designed
    assessment aligned, 95
    consistent, 89, 94
    content standards, 90
    high-level structure, 89–90
    individualized, 96
    integration, 91–92
    learning outcomes varied, 90–91

curriculum, attributes of well-designed *(continued)*
    publicly known, 89
    skills development, 90–91

data collection, 29–30, 139–142, 141–142*f*, 143*f*,
    145*f*, 146*f*
Deal, T. E., 45
decision making skills, 29–30
decisiveness, leadership skill of, 38–39
Dewey, John, 16
Diamond, J. B., 18
discipline policies, 69

Elmore, Richard, 20, 21
Elm Ridge school, 5–6
Enhancing Professional Practice (Danielson), 100
enthusiasm in leadership, 37
evidence. *See* data collection
expectations role in achievement, 52–54, 128

facilitation skills, 134–137
family, involving, 6, 49, 105–110, 111*f*
flexibility, leadership skill of, 39
Fullan, Michael, 13, 18

gender role in class participation, 6–10
grading policies, 71–72
group process tools, 133–137

Halverson, R., 18
hard work
    of change, 9–10
    leadership and, 40
    student learning and, 52–54
Hargreaves, Andy, 17–18
Holtschlag, Margaret, 3–4
homework policies, 70–71
humility in leadership, 37–38
Hunter, Madeline, 98

initiative in leadership, 30
instruction. *See* curriculum, attributes of well-
    designed; teaching

Jackson, D. Bruce, 54
Japanese lesson study, 102

Kallick, Bena, 36
Katzenmeyer, M., 21

leadership, administrative, 16–18, 20–21, 41–44,
    126–127, 129–130. *See also* teacher leadership
leadership dispositions. *See also* teacher leadership
    commitment, 36–37
    confidence, 38–39
    courage, 38
    creativity, 39
    decisiveness, 38–39
    enthusiasm, 37
    flexibility, 39
    humility, 37–38
    open-mindedness, 37–38
    optimism, 37
    perseverance, 40
    risk-taking, 38
    tolerance for ambiguity, 39
    willingness to work hard, 40
leadership skills. *See also* collegiality; teacher
  leadership
    action initiated, 31–33
    adjusts to change, 33–34
    collaboration, 133–134
    commitment, 42
    confidence building, 42
    contributing to the profession, 35–36
    decision making, 29–30
    evaluation, 142–144, 145*f*
    evidence collection, 29–30, 139–142,
        141–142*f*, 143*f*, 145*f*, 146*f*
    facilitation, 134–137
    goal setting, 143
    ideas clarification, 42
    initiative, 30
    negativity anticipated, 34–35
    opportunities recognized, 30
    people mobilized, 30–31
    persuasion, 31, 34–35, 87
    in planning, 137–142, 143*f*
    professional development for, 129
    progress monitored, 33–34
    reflection, 33
    resources obtained, 31–33, 43
    supportive, 34–35
    vision maintenance, 41
learning communities, 15. *See also* student learning
Lewis, Catherine, 102
licensing, 24
Lieberman, A., 23
Little, J. W., 23

looping concept, 5–6

mentoring, 119
Miller, L., 23
minority enrollment in AP classes, 6–10
Moller, G., 21

National Board for Professional Teaching Standards, 24
negotiated agreements, 23–24

open-mind, leadership and an, 37–38
optimism, leadership skill of, 37

parents. *See* family, involving
perseverance, leadership skill of, 34, 40
persuasion, leadership skill of, 31, 34–35, 87
Peterson, K. D., 45
planning, leadership skill of, 137–142, 143*f*
principals. *See* leadership: administrative
privacy norms in creating change, 104
professional development, 24, 80–81, 117–118, 129
professional inquiry, culture of, 54–57, 86

race, role in academic advancement, 6–10
recognition of teacher leaders, 25
reflection, leadership skill of, 33
resources, obtaining, 31–33, 43
respect
    leadership and, 38
    in school culture, 46–51, 127–128
responsibility and student culture, 52–54
risk-taking, leadership skill of, 38, 126–127

school audit, 131–132, 147–153
school-community partnerships, 115, 117–121, 122*f*
school culture
    of independence/autonomy, 55
    influence of, 45–46, 57
    inhibiting leadership, 129–131
    of professional inquiry, 54–57, 86
    promoting leadership, 126–128
    a respectful, 46–51, 127–128
    role in learning, 51–53
    school audit of, 148–149, 150–153*f*
    school structures supporting, 65–66
    student policies and, 72–73

school culture (*continued*)
    for student success, 52–54
school governance, 65–66, 110, 128, 148
schools, communication within/between, 110, 112–115, 116*f*
school structure
    attendance policies, 68–69
    discipline policies, 69
    grading policies, 71–72
    grouping of students, 64
    homework policies, 70–71
    inhibiting teacher leadership, 132
    master schedule, 63–64
    policies and programs, 61–62
    promoting teacher leadership, 128–129
    school audit, 148–149, 150–153*f*
    staff programs, 77, 79–82
    student policies, 66–73
    student programs and activities, 73–77
    subunits, 62–63
Spillane, J., 18
staff, noninstructional, 50
standards, meeting, 13–14, 24–25
Standards for School Leaders (Council of Chief State School Officers), 17
state regulations, meeting, 24
student learning
    expectations role in, 52–54, 71, 90
    results focus on, 85–87
    role of leadership in, 22–23
    school vision for, 51–53
students
    assignment to groups, 64–65
    attendance policies, 68–69
    college classes for, 115, 117
    community service by, 76–77
    discipline policies, 69
    extra- and co-curricular activities, 75
    family involvement in education, 6, 49, 105–110, 111*f*
    grading policies, 71–72
    homework policies, 70–71
    internships for, 119
    as leaders, 75–76
    mentoring of, 119
    policy compliance, methods of, 68
    programs and activities for, 73–77, 78–79*f*
    respectful interactions with, 46–48
student survey, 149, 150*f*

sustainability, 17–18

tall poppy syndrome, 130
teacher leaders
    administrative role of, 41–44
    characteristics of, 12–13, 15, 28
    compensation for, 24
    dispositions, 36–41
    emergence of, 19, 24–25
    influence on instruction, 25, 84–85
    modeling hard work, 54
    professional development role, 81
    recognition of, 25
    reluctance in, 130–131
    skills of, 28–36, 133–137
    social involvement by, 82, 110
teacher leadership. *See also* leadership dispositions;
  leadership skills
    background (concept of), 13–16, 23
    cultivating, 131–132, 147–153
    defined, 12
    effective, creating, 19
    formal roles vs., 18–19, 24–25
    framework for demonstrating, 25–27, 26*f*
    methods of demonstrating, 59–60
    obstacles to, 23–25, 104, 129–131
    purpose of, 134
    state regulations, meeting by, 24
    support factors, 125–129
teacher leadership, examples of
    BIG lesson concept, 3–4
    communication with other educators, 115, 116*f*
    community partnerships, 122*f*
    curriculum examined, 93*f*
    enrollment patterns in AP courses, 6–10
    family involvement in education, 107, 110, 111*f*
    focus on results, 87, 88*f*
    improving instructional practices, 103*f*
    looping concept, 5–6
    problem recognition, 128, 138–139
    schoolwide structures refined, 67*f*

teacher leadership, examples of *(continued)*
    staff programs, 82, 83*f*
    student assessment modeled, 98*f*
    student policy development, 74*f*
    student programs and activities, 75, 77, 78–79*f*
teachers. *See also* collegiality
    academic partnerships, 118–119
    business partnerships, 119
    communication strategies, 110, 112–115, 116*f*
    community service by, 120–121
    de-privatization of practice, 85–86
    evaluation of, 81–82
    experienced, leadership inclinations of, 14–15
    in formal leadership roles, 18–19
    mentoring and coaching of, 81, 102–103, 103*f*
    public perception of, 13
    recruitment and hiring, 79–80
    responsibilities outside the classroom, 101–102,
      105
    school governance participation, 16
    social programs for, 82
    standards for, 13–14, 24
    student group assignment, 64–65
teacher survey, 149, 151–153*f*
teaching. *See also* curriculum, attributes of well-
  designed
    classroom environment and, 101
    framework for, 100–102
    improving instructional practices, 102–103,
      103*f*
    involving students family, 105–110, 111*f*
    parents, 109
    planning and preparation in, 101
    professionalization of, 22–23, 127–128
    standards of practice, 97–100

universities
    school communication with, 114–115
    school partnerships, 115, 117–118, 122*f*
Urbanski, Adam, 40

About the Author

Charlotte Danielson is an education consultant in Princeton, New Jersey. She has taught at all levels, from kindergarten through college; worked as a consultant on curriculum planning, performance assessment, and professional development for numerous schools and districts in the United States and overseas; and designed materials and training programs for Association for Supervision and Curriculum Development, Educational Testing Service, and the National Board for Professional Teaching Standards. She is the author of *Enhancing Student Achievement* (2002), *Enhancing Professional Practice* (1996), and the coauthor with Tom McGreal of *Teacher Evaluation to Enhance Professional Practice* (2000). Danielson may be reached by e-mail at charlotte_danielson@hotmail.com.